To Miss Nellie Repel.

as a token of esteem, and
of gratitude for assistance
rendered in the preparation
of this work for the press.

[illegible]

Athens. April 25. 1877.

CHAPTERS

ON

SCHOOL SUPERVISION

A Practical Treatise on Superintendence; Grading; Arranging Courses of Study; The Preparation and Use of Blanks, Records, and Reports; Examinations for Promotion, Etc.

BY

WILLIAM H. PAYNE, M. A.

Sup't of the Public Schools of Adrian, Mich.

WILSON, HINKLE & CO.

137 Walnut Street
CINCINNATI

28 Bond Street
NEW YORK

ELECTROTYPED AT
FRANKLIN TYPE FOUNDRY
CINCINNATI

ECLECTIC PRESS
WILSON, HINKLE & CO.
CINCINNATI

Non viribus aut velocitatibus aut celeritate corporum res magnæ geruntur, sed CONSILIO, AUCTORITATE, SENTENTIA.

* * * *gubernatorem in navigando nihil agere dicant, quum alii malos scandant, alii per foros cursent, alii sentinam exhauriant,* ILLE AUTEM CLAVUM TENENS SEDEAT IN PUPPI QUIETUS.

Cic., de Senec. vi.

PREFACE.

Every man is a debtor to his profession. At the outset of his career, the current practice which he adopts is an inheritance left him by his professional ancestry; and this, in turn, is to be transmitted to the next generation with such additions as his own industry, sagacity, and thrift, have been able to accumulate during a life of professional toil. Science grows by the increments—insignificant, perhaps, in themselves—which individual experience contributes to the common stock; and no one has a moral right to leave the world without taking care to assure to posterity the net results of a life devoted to a special pursuit.

The profession of teaching has not enjoyed a profusion of such legacies. While men in other professions willingly contribute the results of their matured experience to those who are to succeed them, teachers have been slow to render such a service to their professional brethren. Compared with Law, Medicine, and Theology, Teaching is almost without a professional literature. In the other professions named, not only is there a vast collection of practical works, the recorded results of individual experience, but there are numerous treatises on the history and philosophy of the several sciences—attempts to collate the great facts in each art, and to deduce from them certain first principles which may serve to prepare the way for a more rational practice. Of works of the first class there are but comparatively few to which teachers may have access; while of the second class there is scarcely a single example, in English, which, with any propriety, can be called a treatise on the philosophy of education. The great law of the division of labor has called into existence a new class of professional men, whose duty is the supervision of schools and school systems; yet, up to this time, no work, not even the most elementary, has been published on an art whose importance can scarcely be over-estimated.

The present work is offered as a contribution to the practical literature of teaching. Its general scope and purpose are best explained by remarking that it is a record of experience. The plans and suggestions which it embodies were not inspired by mere theories of what ought to be, or of what might be, but are the results which have been reached in the course of a considerable experience in the management of schools. It is not meant by this that all the plans herein contained are original; on the contrary, many of them have come, either by suggestion or adoption, from the current practice in school supervision. The writer will scarcely be robbed of any credit which really belongs to him, if the reader is left to infer that this book merely presents an outline of the practice which is current in our best graded-schools.

It is due alike to the reader, the writer, and the critic, to state that this treatise is written from a particular point of view,—that of a superintendent of a school system such as is found in the smaller cities of this country. I do not presume to write for the instruction of those who superintend the school systems of our larger cities. Having had no experience in work of such magnitude and complexity, I have no fitness for giving advice as to the doing of this variety of school-work.

I am not aware that a work of this special character has ever been presented to the public; and, as it has been composed without models to follow, it will, no doubt, be easy to base a just criticism both on its matter and its method. If it serve no other good purpose, it will, I hope, stimulate abler hands to execute a similar undertaking, more worthy of the profession whose interests it is designed to promote.

The doctrines which are embodied in this work are expressed with the utmost frankness, yet not, I hope, with any thing which borders on dogmatism. Freely granting to all men the right to express their opinions with freedom and emphasis, I here claim a similar right to express my convictions on some disputed questions in educational policy. I see very clearly that some of the opinions which are here embodied will meet with a hearty protest in many candid minds; but, while I can not hope that the general line of policy which I have attempted to set forth will be acceptable to all, I think I may, without impropriety, bespeak that judicial fairness which dares to weigh opinions at variance with cherished convictions.

One remark may save the author from misinterpretation and the reader from possible mistakes. In all that relates to practical school-work, such as grading, tabulating courses of study, arranging programmes, etc., etc., the aim has been chiefly to illustrate the general principles which should be observed. In actual practice such modifications must be made as peculiar circumstances may require.

I take pleasure in acknowledging my indebtedness to Superintendents Doty, Rickoff, and Harris for some of the forms included in this volume. Others have been prepared expressly for this work, and are the exclusive property of the Publishers.

W. H. PAYNE.

ADRIAN, MICH.,
Aug. 1, 1875.

CONTENTS.

BLANKS AND FORMS.

N. B.—Many of these forms are copyrighted, and are the property of the publishers.

CHAPTER I.

THE NATURE AND VALUE OF SUPERINTENDENCE.

SUMMARY.

Mental energy and muscular energy. Human society a hierarchy of forces. The highest forms of labor often undervalued. The highest form of labor that which involves the expenditure of the highest form of force. Division of labor a law of human progress. Civilization a process of differentiation. Division of labor as applied to education. A school system requires direction by one responsible head. Two varieties of labor are required in every systematized industry. Empiricism in teaching. The reign of law. The science of education. Educational science in Great Britain. The need of school supervision not every-where acknowledged. The responsibility of superintendents.

THE NATURE AND VALUE OF SUPERINTENDENCE.

1. **Mental energy and muscular energy.**—The hand and the brain both toil. Each has its appointed office to fulfill, and each is entitled to a consideration proportionate to the quality of the service which it renders. The energy which is expended in lifting and pounding has its measurable value; and the mental power which determines the nature and amount of muscular activity has its value. But these values are not the same, and are not measurable by the same standard. The human organism is the seat of a hierarchy of forces. Some are appointed to command, others to obey; some are employed in devising plans, others in executing them; some work in silence, far removed from sensual observation, others are obtrusive and give ceaseless evidence of their existence. Mental energy and muscular energy have their respective values. Each is indispensable in the economy of nature, and each is to be valued according to its rank in the hierarchy to which it belongs.

2. **Human society a hierarchy of forces.**—Human society is also a hierarchy of forces. Organization implies subordination. If there is to be a plan, some one must devise it, while others must execute it. As the members of the human body execute the behests of the supreme in-

telligence, so in human society the many must follow the direction of the few. It is not possible to conceive a state of society in which there are not inequalities based on gradations in the ability to govern. For one man who can design a house, there are a thousand who are able only to lay the brick and the stone as they are directed. For one man competent to plan a military campaign, there are myriads of soldiers whose province is to obey the orders of their commanders. Human society is organized on the principle that the weak are to be protected by the strong, the improvident by the provident, and the masses of mankind voluntarily submit to the guidance of those who have the faculty of directing.

3. **The highest forms of labor often undervalued.**—The energy which is expended in supervision, in direction, in government, is not always estimated at its just value. In general we estimate the value of labor by the amount of demonstration which accompanies it. The sailor who climbs the mast, who furls the sail, and who heaves out the bilge-water, seems a more useful man than the helmsman who scarcely moves a muscle of his body. So accustomed are we to measure all things by the impressions which they make on our senses, that we are slow to acknowledge the supreme importance of those imponderable forces which really govern and direct. The thunder terrifies, and so Jupiter Tonans is worshiped and propitiated. It was left to a later and a wiser agc to discover that the agent which blasts and kills is as imponderable as thought. Men, too, are inclined to measure all labor by a reference to their own experience. Agricola, who sweats as he toils, and is covered with the dust which his own violent exertions have raised, can scarcely realize that Clericus, cool-browed and clean, is at all worthy of a laborer's hire.

4. The highest form of labor that which involves the expenditure of the highest form of force.—But the highest form of labor is that which is attended with the expenditure of the highest form of force. Between muscular energy and mental energy, the antithesis is too striking to be overlooked; but different orders of intellectual power may give their possessors unequal spheres of usefulness, and may therefore entitle them to unequal rates of compensation. Abilities may be ranked according to their relative comprehensiveness. The commanding general, who, at one glance, takes in the whole military situation, and wields his forces so as to meet the exigencies of the situation, is the natural superior of the thousands who, with powers of mind less comprehensive, merely execute the plans prescribed by their leader. The highest forms of labor, therefore, are those which involve the expenditure of the highest forms of energy.

5. Division of labor a law of human progress.—That distribution of labor which characterizes our higher civilization has established system and method in every branch of human industry. Where the several portions of a complicated process are assigned to special hands, a general plan must bind together the related parts, and secure their harmonious and efficient action; and back of this plan there must be an intelligence to coördinate and control. He who secures uniformity, accuracy, and harmony in a complicated industrial process, imparts additional value to the products of each man's toil. Superintendence is therefore not only a necessity, but is the highest and most productive form of labor.

6. Civilization a process of differentiation.—Civilization is a process of differentiation. Rude tribes are homogeneous with respect to their industrial state. There is no division of labor whereby each man devotes himself to that pursuit in which he has the most skill. But as civilization advances, occupations become more and more diverse, as men restrict themselves to industries more and more specific. In new settlements, a tradesman sells hardware, groceries, dry-goods, medicines, boots and shoes, etc.; but as population increases, and other tradesmen come into competition with him, he restricts himself to a single branch of trade, in which he is specially skilled. In the tribal condition of mankind, the same man is priest, lawgiver, physician, and teacher; but soon there is a separation of functions, each man devoting his attention to the pursuit for which he has the greatest aptitude. As the priest was the most learned man in early communities, he was also the teacher; and the first schools were connected with places of religious worship. The church has ever been the foster-parent of the school; and Christianity has signalized her conquests by founding institutions of learning. Gradually, however, the work of instruction has been relegated to laymen, and teaching has become a secular employment. But traditions are slow to disappear, and even now it is rare to find a college president who is not a clergyman, and there are few schools in which there are not religious observances of some description.

7. Division of labor as applied to education.— Isolated schools may meet the requirements of a sparse population; but in highly civilized and populous communities, the work of instruction follows the great law of the division of labor, and different portions are assigned to those who have special aptitudes. It is soon discovered that children are best taught in a school by themselves: and if the number of pupils is sufficiently large, the adults are assigned to one teacher; those who are younger, to a second; and the mere children, to a third. Thus there arises the idea of grades, based primarily on age, and finally on acquirements. Farther than this, certain branches of instruction are assigned, as specialties, to teachers who have a peculiar fitness for giving instruction in them. Pupils thus classified by age and attainments, and taught by those who are specially fitted for restricted portions of the work of instruction, constitute a Graded-School, or a system of such schools.

8. A school system requires direction by one responsible head.— It is thus seen that the work of instruction follows the law which prevails in all other industries—differentiation, classification, system; and, as in a complicated process of manufacture, while each workman is held responsible for that part which he executes, some one man is held responsible for the general result; so in an extended system of instruction there should be a responsible head, able to devise plans in general and in detail, and vested with sufficient authority to keep all subordinates in their proper places, and at their assigned tasks. A graded-school of a thousand pupils and twenty teachers involves a system of great complexity, and requires the nicest adjustments in order to work with harmony and efficiency. The arrangement of courses of study, the examination and classification of pupils, their discipline and correction, the oversight of teachers, the compilation of records—these are some of the items on which depends the success of the system, and which require the attention of a single responsible head.

9. Two varieties of labor required in every systematized industry.—Two varieties of labor are required in every occupation—that of planning and that of executing. Most men work after prescribed rules. It is easier to follow the footsteps of others than to beat a new path for ourselves. Some, however, are most naturally and successfully employed in organizing, planning, and supervising. This difference is constitutional. While most men are content to know how a process is performed, a comparatively few are impelled to study the *rationale* of methods. In other words, there is empirical knowledge and scientific knowledge—a knowledge of processes merely, and a profounder knowledge of the laws which underlie these processes. The engineer who drives his engine merely from imitation, and the engineer who understands the construction of this wonderful machine and the mechanical principles which are involved in its working, possess two widely different grades of qualifications. The first is a machine in charge of a machine; to the other, the engine is as though it were transparent, revealing its minutest part, and wholly subject to his directing will. In case of accident, these two orders of knowledge are brought into striking contrast. The lower knowledge is useless in times of derangement—under abnormal circumstances; while the higher, being able to penetrate into the causes of disturbance, may restore the normal situation of affairs. The peculiar value of scientific knowledge is the extent of its previsions—previsions which may be employed either in anticipating and providing against disaster, or in devising new and better processes.

10. Empiricism in teaching.—It is safe to say that there is no profession in which empiricism prevails to such an extent as in teaching. In other professions there is a course of preparatory training, designed to unfold the scientific principles which underlie the arts in question; and in actual practice there is constant reference to the laws which are involved in the various cases presenting themselves, and an effort to discover the causes of that which is abnormal, and thus to proceed by rational methods. In teaching, however, tradition and imitation are dominant. In this country, at least, teaching is for the most part a mechanical employment, and teachers differ from one another chiefly in industry and tact. To superintend the work of instruction with advantage requires, at least, considerable executive ability, a somewhat complete knowledge of the branches taught, and ready skill in discipline. With these qualifications alone, a system of instruction may be kept from deteriorating, but it is not likely that it will be improved to any considerable extent—improved, that is, by the conception of more philosophic methods, and the skillful adaptation of means to desired ends. What is involved in an improvement purposely made? A close scrutiny of the principles involved; an ideal scheme of what is desirable; and an intelligent employment of adequate means. The improvement is first constructed in thought, by "the scientific use of the imagination," and then the plan is patiently embodied in practice. Superintendence, then, requires, in addition to practical skill, scientific prevision derived from a profounder knowledge of the science of education.

11. **The reign of law.**—A characteristic feature of modern thought is the extension which has been given to the province of law. Formerly, physical phenomena alone were thought subject to the laws of cause and effect, while vast domains of nature were relegated to the caprices of chance; but now, social phenomena and mental phenomena, the organization of society and the creations of the intelligence are admitted to be under the reign of law. If, even now, certain classes of phenomena can not be explained by bringing them under higher generalizations, it is not because they are not cases of a general law, but because the network is so complicated that human ingenuity has hitherto

been unable to unravel it; yet it is certain that the whole current of modern thought is setting steadily in the direction of extending the domain of law, and hence of scientific prevision. It is thus that each art has its correlative science; that is, each process is recognized as depending on definite laws of cause and effect, a knowledge of which will serve to account for failures and to open up the way for studied improvements.

12. The science of education.—Along with the discovery that mental phenomena may be explained by referring them to the general laws which regulate the processes of thinking, feeling, and willing, there has dawned the idea that education is not merely an imitative art, but that, in fact, it rests on an ascertainable basis of law, and that its processes may be perfected by bringing them into harmony with nature. While this conception is slowly gaining ground, educational methods are still chiefly empirical; teaching is, for the most part, an art without principles,—a handicraft exercised from convenience or from necessity. To be ennobled, an art must offer free scope to the exercise of the intellect; the trained hand must derive fresh accessions of skill from the cultivated brain. Education is waiting to be thus ennobled; and coming generations should be trained by the skill of teachers who are able to adapt means to desired ends, through a knowledge of the laws which underlie the unfoldings of the human intelligence, and even the assertions of the human will; and if the great army of teachers must follow prescribed methods, they should be led by those who are master workmen, versed both in the theory and practice of teaching. How shall our educational methods be regenerated? How shall they be subjected to revision and correction? By what standard shall novel methods be tested? These queries disclose the need of recognized first principles to which we may refer for proof of the validity of our methods, and by the light of which we may place the art of teaching in that course of progress which characterizes all other professions. Facilities should be given for the cultivation of this new science, and for bringing its truths to bear on the current practice of teaching. Superintendents of schools should be the apostles of this new gospel, and should preach its truths to those who depend on them for guidance.

13. **Educational science in Great Britain.**—There is reason to think that an educational philosophy is now in process of formation, and that, ere long, there will be a rational escape from many of the uncertainties, absurdities, and embarrassments which now beset all varieties of school work. The following extract from a recent number of *The Popular Science Monthly* gives evidence of the direction in which educational thought in Great Britain is moving.

"One of the most important papers read in the Section of Economic Science of the British Association was that by Mrs. Gray on the 'Science of Education.' The author complained that in Britain there is no adequate or general conception of what education is, and, therefore, of the magnitude and complexity of the facts on which a science of education, which can never be an exact, but only a mixed and applied science, must be based. We start with a confusion of terms, using education as synonymous with instruction; and the confusion of thought indicated by this misnomer runs through our whole treatment of the subject. It is surely time that this confusion should be replaced by a scientific conception of the process which should result in the most valuable of all products,—human beings developed to the full extent of their natural capacity. What is wanted is that teachers, like practical navigators, should be furnished with the principles of a science they have not had to discover for themselves, and with charts to guide their general course, leaving to their individual acumen the adaptations and modifications required by special circumstances. We have such knowledge to guide us in improving our breeds of cattle and our crops. Must we remain without it in the infinitely more important business of improving our human crop, of getting out of our human soil all that it can be made to yield for social and individual good? Must every tyro still be allowed to try experiments, not *in corpore vili*, but on the most delicate and precious of materials—the human body and mind—in the most powerful of all forces—human passions and the human will; experiments in which success or failure means virtue or vice, happiness or misery, lives worthy or unworthy; sowing with every action a seed of good or ill, to reproduce itself in an endless series beyond all human ken?"

14. **The need of school supervision not everywhere acknowledged.**—It is an anomalous fact that while all men freely acknowledge the need of enlightened supervision in mechanical employments, in trade, and in government, there is often extreme reluctance to admit its value and necessity in the management of school systems. Men who themselves are most usefully employed in directing the affairs of a printing-office, of a book-store, or of a foundry, will deny to a school the right of having a responsible head. Nor is it difficult to account for this reluctance. First, there is the general fact that teaching is not generally regarded as an art having processes of its own, requiring skill of a special kind, and needing special preparation for its duties. In the view of all who have formed this notion of teaching, the man who is charged with the duty of supervising the work of instruction is a supernumerary. Then there is the special fact that, as yet, there has not been a clear differentiation between teaching and superintendence.

The fact that superintendence requires a different kind of knowledge, perhaps a higher order of knowledge, is not generally admitted. And thus it is that even if some oversight is deemed to be requisite, it is assumed that it can be exercised in an unofficial capacity by the Board of Education or by some one of the regular teaching force. The real fact is, as I have attempted to show, that the complicated structure of a graded system of instruction requires a constant oversight by one responsible head, able to direct the movements of the whole system, and vested with sufficient authority to enforce, if necessary, a compliance with his decisions; and, further, that, in response to this need, the law of the division of labor has called into existence, out of the teaching class, a new body of professional men who differ from teachers as an architect differs from the workmen who follow the plan which he has prescribed.

15. The responsibility of superintendents. — By that inherent law of progress whereby vocations are specialized, the active administration of city and village school systems has been intrusted to superintendents and principals. Though not authorized to expend a dollar of public funds on their own authority, they virtually direct the outlay of a large portion of the moneys raised for educational purposes. By common consent, superintendents are allowed to have an influential voice in the arrangement of courses of study, in the adoption of text-books, in the selection of teachers, in the purchase of apparatus, in the distribution of work, and, in general, in every important item of school economy. In reality, therefore, the turning point of success in public school affairs is the industry, skill, and good sense of those who are charged with the duty of employing the ways and means which the people so generously supply. It is a discreditable fact that, on the whole, the net results of our public school administration are far below what they ought to be, when considered with reference to the total expense at which they have been secured; and it is a fact still more discreditable that, to a considerable extent, this result is chargeable to the incompetence of those who have the direct supervision of schools — to a lack of professional skill in the performance of the trusts which have been assigned them. In all industries the condition of success is skilled labor — skill in the operative and skill in the oversight of operatives; a skill which uses every item of material to the best purpose, and turns out the greatest amount of the best products. In teaching there is a lack of skilled labor, and especially of that variety of labor which is most truly productive — supervision. It is to an awakened zeal among superintendents and principals that we must look for a body of doctrine which shall introduce rational processes into all departments of school work, and thus make possible an economical use of the resources which a generous people bestow on universal education.

CHAPTER II.

THE SUPERINTENDENT'S POWERS DEFINED AND SOME OF HIS GENERAL DUTIES DISCUSSED.

SUMMARY.

The people may delegate certain powers to a Board of Trustees. A Board of Trustees may assign certain duties to a superintendent of schools. Superintendents and principals. The time which may be profitably devoted to general supervision. A superintendent should not be subject to interference in the discharge of his professional duties. The classification of pupils. The selection of teachers. The examination of teachers. The sources from which graded-schools may derive their teachers.

THE SUPERINTENDENT'S POWERS AND DUTIES.

16. The people may delegate certain powers to a Board of Trustees. — When the people have chosen a certain number of men, as their representatives, to administer a portion of their interests, a virtual contract has been made whereby these interests have passed for a time from their direct control into the hands of their agents. The powers thus assigned are irrevocable during the period for which these representatives are chosen, or until they are removed from office by impeachment or other legal process. Thus during their term of office the trustees of a school district have the entire administration of school affairs, and are not subject to the dictation of those by whom they were appointed. From the very nature of the representative system, certain limits are assigned to the jurisdiction of school officers; but while acting within these limits, their official action should be dictated only by their own enlightened sense of duty. What end is gained in electing men of superior qualifications to official positions, unless they are granted some independent use of their own wisdom and discretion? Officials should certainly respect the honest convictions of their constituents, but they should as certainly be guided in their official acts by their own convictions of right and duty in all matters which have been intrusted to their care. In case of evident maladministration, the people may obtain legal redress; or if there is dissatisfaction with the manner in which an officer has performed his duties, there is the effectual remedy, at the close of his official term, of choosing his successor. The employment of teachers, the fixing of their salaries, the selection of text-books, the adoption of courses of study, the purchase of libraries and apparatus are among the duties exclusively assigned to boards of trustees; and the integrity and intelligence with which these duties are performed will determine the efficiency and worth of the school system.

17. A Board of Trustees may assign certain duties to a superintendent of schools.—By a further extension of the representative system, a board of trustees having charge of the general educational interests of a community may delegate certain powers and assign corresponding duties to a superintendent of schools; and while acting within the limits of these delegated powers, this officer is as far removed from interference by the board of trustees as the latter is from interference by the people.

In case the superintendent exceeds his prescribed powers, he is removable from office; or in case he does not perform his duties to the satisfaction of his superiors, they have a sufficient remedy in choosing his successor at the expiration of his term of office. The powers conferred on a superintendent of schools are usually determined by the rules and regulations of the governing body; and while there is some variation in the amount of authority given to this officer, his general duties may be stated as follows:

(1) To classify pupils according to their attainments.

(2) To advise the Board of the qualifications of the teachers employed, and to anticipate the vacancies which are likely to occur.

(3) To enforce an observance of the courses of study and the use of the prescribed text-books.

(4) In cases of difficulty, to assist teachers in the discipline of pupils, and to secure an observance of the rules and regulations of the Board.

(5) To prescribe rules for the conduct of pupils in the school buildings and on the school grounds.

(6) To direct teachers in their methods of instruction and discipline.

The superintendent is thus the executive officer of the Board, so far as the internal management of the school is concerned; and whenever circumstances warrant the appointment of a special officer of this kind, his distinctive work will be of the kind just mentioned. For the sake of setting forth the relation, growing out of these requirements, of the superintendent to the governing body under whose orders he acts, and of presenting in their appropriate connection some of the most important subjects pertaining to public school policy, several of the above topics will be discussed at considerable length.

18. Superintendents and Principals. — In the West, where the graded-school system has been quite fully developed, it is usual to appoint a superintendent when the aggregate enrollment is twelve hundred or upward. The tendency is to appoint a special officer in schools considerably smaller; and in many schools of three or four hundred pupils the principal teacher styles himself superintendent. This, however, is a manifest perversion of language. The time of a superintendent is exclusively or very largely employed in the general oversight of teachers and schools: he is rather an officer of the Board than a member of the corps of teachers. The principal teacher in a smaller school, on the other hand, is almost exclusively engaged in teaching, and his legitimate title is Principal. I suspect that this unauthorized use of titles is a weakness somewhat peculiar to the West, where almost every man in charge of a school with one assistant is a "Professor." This fondness for titles very justly exposes the profession of teaching to ridicule, and confounds ideas which should be kept distinct.

When the aggregate enrollment is less than one thousand, the appointment of a superintendent is scarcely justifiable. In such cases, the principal of the school should be relieved from teaching for a part of his time, in order that he may give some attention to general supervision. He may very properly be held responsible for the classification of pupils and for their general discipline. By frequently convening teachers for consultation and instruction, and by occasional visits to their schools, he may secure a very efficient organization. In some instances there is not a clear recognition of a principal's rights and duties; and, in consequence of this, there is danger of unnecessary and mischievous interference in the internal affairs of the school. If a principal is worthy of his position, he is competent to maintain the efficiency of his school; and while held rigidly responsible for results, he should be granted all proper freedom of action. It is a great injustice to exact certain results and yet to withhold means of attaining them. Responsibilities should be commensurate with facilities for meeting them.

At the outset, there should be a distinct understanding as to the limits of the principal's authority. If necessary, let his duties be defined by contract, so that there may be no encroachment by either party on the rights of the other.

19. The time which may be profitably devoted to general supervision.—The amount of time which should be employed in general supervision must be determined by the circumstances in each special case. The only general rule which can be given is, that the head of a school should make his labor as remunerative as possible. The amount of time which may be profitably employed in superintendence will depend on the number of schools, their distance from one another, the degree to which work has been systematized, and the efficiency of the teaching force. The need of supervision is relatively great when there is a large number of schools, when they are scattered over a considerable area, when the system is imperfectly developed, and when teachers are inefficient or inexperienced.

Schools which employ forty teachers require the entire time of a superintendent. Where there are thirty teachers, and the schools are well organized, four-fifths of the superintendent's time should be devoted to general supervision. With twenty teachers, the half of each day is enough for general purposes; and where there are less than ten teachers in one building, not more than one-fifth of a principal's time need be given to supervision. These estimates are based on a normal condition of affairs. Under exceptional circumstances, such as the inauguration of a new system or a considerable number of new teachers, more time will be required for the general oversight of affairs.

It is well to recollect that the ultimate support of our public school system is the well-earned confidence of the people. Good schools will necessarily cost large sums of money. The people have every-where shown themselves willing to be taxed for educational purposes; but it is more than probable that, in the natural course of events, there may be developed a tendency to reaction; and it is hence incumbent on all who are charged with the administration of public school affairs to make all expenditures as remunerative as possible. Should the principal of a school which numbers one thousand pupils spend his entire time in "superintending," it is probable that his employers would soon become disgusted with a system which needed so much watching. Teachers who need such constant oversight can not be economically employed; and there is danger that even good teachers would lose their ability for independent work under such a system.

20. A superintendent has his professional rights.—In cases where the superintendent is exclusively or chiefly occupied in the work of supervision, he should be held rigidly responsible for results, and should be allowed all necessary powers, privileges, and helps. In matters which are entirely within the sphere of his professional duties, he should work without hinderance; in others where there is concurrent authority, there should be conference; in others which are wholly within the prerogatives of the Board, he should not interfere even by suggestion. It is essential to the harmony and efficiency of a school that there be this clear definition of duties and prerogatives; and wherever the line may fall, there should be the most exact observance of all that is implied in the contract. Competent and honorable men are made the better by being trusted. They will accomplish more and better work if confidence is placed in their discretion and ability. If a superintendent can not be trusted to do the work which belongs to his profession, he should be discharged, and the management of the school placed in competent hands.

Nothing is more fatal to the harmonious working of a school system than a misunderstanding of the relative powers and duties of the Board and the superintendent. The Board, as the governing body, should permit no trespass on its exclusive privileges; but, at the same time, there should be left to the superintendent a full scope for the performance of his duties as they may be defined by contract or otherwise. It is not difficult to see how a man, conscious of his ability to do the work required of him, may be annoyed by needless interference; nor how such interference may be a real trespass on his rights. The mere fact that a man is placed in charge of such interests should be a guaranty that, while in the performance of his duties, his professional rights will be respected. When a physician is summoned to the bedside of an invalid, he is for a time invested with certain prerogatives which should shield him from dictation and interference. The fact of his being summoned is a virtual acknowledgment of his competence; and so long as he is in charge of the case, no one has a moral right to dictate his method of practice.

I am the farthest from justifying any mere assumption of dignity, power, or prerogative; but it is clear that a superintendent has some sphere of professional duty, however limited, and that within this sphere he should be trusted to exercise his skill unmolested. In general, these limits are settled by usage; but in cases where this unwritten law has no binding force, a definite understanding should prevent those divisions and disagreements which result so disastrously.

21. **The classification of pupils.**—The duty of placing new pupils in classes where their time can be employed to the greatest advantage, and of making such reclassifications as ability and industry may make necessary, is one of the most important which a Board of Trustees can require of a superintendent. It has been urged as an objection to graded-schools, that sufficient provision is not made for differences in individual ability; that in case a pupil becomes able to do more work than his classmates, it is difficult, if not impossible, to give him a reclassification which will do him exact justice. This objection will be more fully considered in another place (§ 97); and it is mentioned here only to show that it may be removed, to a considerable extent, by

exercising great care in classifying new pupils. For it is plain that when pupils have been once put in their proper places it will not be necessary, save under exceptional circumstances, to give them a reclassification before the close of the year, when there will occur a general readjustment of the school.

It is convenient to distinguish three classes of new pupils.

(1) Those who have never attended any school.

(2) Those who come from graded-schools.

(3) Those who come from ungraded schools.

Nothing needs to be done with applicants of the first class except to place them in the first year of the primary grade.

The classification of pupils who have been instructed in graded-schools is not attended with any special difficulty. Such is the general uniformity in graded courses of instruction that a pupil may easily pass from one classified school to another and take up his work where it had been dropped.

The work done in ungraded schools is usually unsymmetrical. As studies are selected with but little regard to their natural order and intrinsic importance, it usually happens that there is considerable proficiency in some branches, while others, of the same grade, are almost wholly neglected. The direct result of this is, that, at the outset, it is impossible to give pupils who have been instructed in this unsystematic manner a rational classification. Proficiency in reading, or in arithmetic, may entitle them to enter one of the higher grades, while a relatively poor knowledge of grammar or of geography may make it necessary to classify them with pupils who are considerably younger. As a general rule, pupils who come from ungraded schools must be classed somewhat lower than those who have been taught in graded-schools; but by reason of their age and greater maturity they will often make more rapid progress than their classmates, and may require, in consequence, a reclassification. As the first classification of such pupils must be, to some extent, provisional, it is best, in general, to anticipate the probable need of a reclassification, by placing them among pupils who are somewhat their superiors in point of scholarship. Even if, in spite of this precaution, they outgrow their first classification, the ability which has enabled them to attain this result will permit their transfer to a higher grade.

In deciding on a pupil's fitness for admission, it is of the utmost importance to take into consideration his general ability. This ability, though depending primarily on innate mental habit, may also depend on health, industry, and acquired habits of study. Generally, older pupils have a maturity of mind which will enable them to accomplish more work than their younger classmates; but it will not be safe to take this for granted in all cases. If it is discovered that a pupil of limited acquirements has a mind of more than ordinary activity and power of comprehension, there need be no hesitation in giving him a higher classification than his mere literary attainments would justify. In all cases where it is impossible to classify a pupil of good ability with exactness, it is better to place him with superiors than with inferiors. Some margin should be allowed for the exercise of a pupil's reserve force.

In making examinations for promotion, there is less occasion to inquire into a pupil's latent ability, since this has been transformed into actual acquirement. If a graded system of instruction is wisely administered, a pupil's ability, whether based on mental habit, health, or industry, will be concretely represented in his final standing.

22. The selection of teachers.—As the general success of a school depends very largely on the quality of its teaching force, and as the superintendent is expected to secure efficient instruction and discipline throughout all departments, it seems wholly reasonable that he should have some voice in the selection of teachers. In this matter the Board and superintendent should act concurrently. While the latter has no right to employ teachers on his own authority, it is certainly right that his opinion of their fitness should be respected. It is conceivable that, through favoritism, he may recommend those who are unfit; or, through unworthy motives, may stand in the way of those who are deserving; but there is an effectual remedy for this evil, in a change of superintendent.

On the other hand, by confiding, to some extent, the selection of teachers to his judgment, he is made to feel a personal interest in their success, as a failure would be a direct reflection on his sagacity and general ability. Besides, when teachers know that their positions depend in some measure on his estimate of their fitness, they will apply themselves the more earnestly to the execution of his plans. There must be some relation between subordinate teachers and their superior, whereby there shall be prompt obedience to authority; and there seems to be no more natural bond than that which results from the fact that positions are dependent somewhat on the will of the superintendent. It should be remarked, also, that there is no duty more beset with difficulties and embarrassments than that of being obliged to report the deficiencies of teachers to the governing body; and yet this duty, all important as it is, can not be reasonably exacted, unless the right of exercising some choice in the selection of teachers is conceded.

23. The examination of teachers. — Great caution should be exercised in the selection of teachers. Their literary qualifications should be ascertained with great care. When schools are organized under special acts, the examination of teachers will devolve on the Board, or on the Committee on Teachers and Schools. The actual examinations are usually conducted by the superintendent, acting under the authority of the Board. These examinations should not be technical, calculated to exhibit the wisdom and shrewdness of the examiners, but should be designed to test the accuracy and extent of the teacher's knowledge. An examination by writing is preferable, because there will be exhibited some important items, such as penmanship, spelling, punctuation, and practical grammar, which would not sufficiently appear in an oral examination. Besides, the results of an examination conducted in this manner will form a permanent record, to which reference may be made in time of need. These papers should be marked as in an examination of pupils for promotion (§ 111); and the applicants should be ranked, so far as their literary qualifications are concerned, according to the average value of their papers.

But while a certain degree of text-book knowledge is indispensable, this of itself is not sufficient to determine the fitness of an applicant for a situation. Literary ability is but one factor in the conditions of success. The amount of experience which candidates have had, their health, their manners, are all items of importance which should be taken into consideration. Yet excellence in all the points above named will not form a real teacher, unless there is an added quality which gives tone to the whole character—studentship.

Education should be an inspiration; and unless teachers themselves are enthusiastic students, they can not inspire their pupils with a love for books and study. A man whose present attainments are limited, but who is brimful of enthusiasm for reading and study, is a hundredfold more likely to become a successful teacher than a man with a better furnished mind who has lost his zeal for intellectual pursuits. A steady growth in knowledge and culture should be required of every teacher; and when it is known that one is passing his time in intellectual sloth, he should be made to give place to another who is worthy of preferment.

Teachers who satisfy the requirements made of them should receive a certificate to that effect, which qualifies them to become candidates for vacancies which may occur. A book of blank certificates, drawn up in the form of that on page 39, will furnish an exact and convenient record of the examinations, and of candidates who are eligible to positions.

In order to estimate the comparative literary ability of candidates, it is desirable that each applicant should answer the same series of questions. Whenever it becomes necessary, a second series of the same scope may be substituted for the first.

The following list of questions is intended to suggest the form of a written examination, suitable for ordinary use:

State your name, age, the length of time you have taught, and whether you have made any special preparation for the business of teaching.

(1) What works have you read on general literature, science, and mental philosophy?

(2) What method of teaching children to read do you prefer? What are the grounds of your preference?

(3) What objects would you seek to accomplish in the ordinary reading exercise?

(4) How would you first instruct children in counting, adding, and subtracting?

Name ....

Age ....

Experience ....

SCHOLARSHIP.

Reading	....
Writing	....
Spelling	....
Grammar	....
Arithmetic	....
Geography	....
History	....
Physiology	______
Average	....

Period of License ....

Date 187

The Public Schools of ____________________

TEACHER'S CERTIFICATE.

This Certifies that we have examined ____________________ *in Reading, Writing, Spelling, Grammar, Arithmetic, Geography, History, and Physiology; and we hereby license* ________ *to teach in the Public Schools of this City for the period of* ____________

____
____________________ } EXAMINERS.
____

____________ 187 ____________________ SUPT.

(5) Name the first eight periods in their order.

(6) Explain the subtracting of 5682 from 9007.

(7) Add the fractions $\frac{2}{3}$, $\frac{5}{7}$, $\frac{8}{9}$, $\frac{3}{14}$, and $\frac{7}{12}$.

(8) Divide $\frac{7}{8}$ by $\frac{4}{5}$ and analyze the process.

(9) If $3\frac{1}{3}$ yards of cloth cost $7\frac{1}{5}$ dollars, how many yards can be bought for $20\frac{3}{4}$ dollars?

(10) What is the difference between a common fraction and a decimal fraction?

(11) State the process of dividing one decimal fraction by another.

(12) At six and one-fourth cents each, how many oranges can be bought for seven dollars and twenty cents?

(13) Sold sugar at $12\frac{1}{2}$ cents per pound, and lost 25 per cent. What was its cost?

(14) Compute the interest on $325.52, for 2 years, 7 months, and 18 days, at 7 per cent.

(15) Explain the cause of the change of seasons.

(16) Why is the tropic of Cancer $23\frac{1}{2}$ degrees from the equator?

(17) Give the location and width of the zones.

(18) Through what waters must a vessel pass in sailing from Chicago to London?

(19) Describe the principal river systems of North America.

(20) In what states, and in what direction from Chicago, are the following cities? Rochester, Lowell, New Haven, Columbia, Detroit, St. Louis, Montgomery, San Francisco.

(21) Name the principal countries of Europe and their capitals.

(22) Parse the words which are numbered in the following: "[1]Lord, be pleased to [2]shake [3]my clay cottage [4]before thou [5]throwest it [6]down. May it [7]totter awhile before [8]it doth tumble. [9]Let me be [10]summoned before I [11]am surprised. Deliver me [12]from sudden death. [13]Not from [14]sud-

den death in [15]respect of itself, [16]for I care not [17]how [18]short my passage [19]be, so it be [20]safe. [21]But let it not [22]be sudden in respect [23]of me."

(23) Give the principal parts of the following verbs: Go, do, bring, think, sing, run, dream, ring, buy, eat.

(24) Arrange the following in the form of blank verse: "Again the genius of old Rome shall from the dust uprear his reverĕnd head, rous'd by the shout of millions, then before his high tribunal thou and I appear."

(25) Name the principal historians, novelists, and poets of America.

(26) What causes led to the Revolution, the War of 1812, and the Rebellion?

(27) Name the thirteen original states.

(28) Name the Presidents of the United States in their order.

(29) State the manner in which an election for President takes place.

(30) How are Senators and Representatives chosen, and for what period?

(31) By what process is the blood purified by respiration?

(32) How is the air of a school-room made unfit for use?

(33) What precautions should be employed in regulating the temperature and purity of the air in school-rooms?

(34) Explain the working of a common pump.

(35) A cubic foot of water weighs 1,000 ounces. How many cubic feet will a ton of iron occupy, its specific gravity being 7.3?

These questions will doubtless offend by their simplicity. They are intended as a protest against the popular theory of "exhaustive" examinations. Let it be recollected that, at best, the answers to examination questions are but exponents of what is known on certain topics. It is evidently impossible to devise a series of questions which shall exhibit all the knowledge which a teacher has on a special subject. The best we can do is to establish certain data from which we may infer the extent of the candidate's knowledge. Thus, we may presume that a teacher who can give a clear analysis of the reduction of a complex fraction has a competent knowledge of common fractions; while ignorance on this point is not only of itself a partial disqualification, but it involves an ignorance of the general subject. What seems desirable in a written examination is to bring into sharp outline certain portions of knowledge which involve an acquaintance with facts and principles of a lower order. If the purpose be to enter upon a minute examination into isolated facts, it will be best secured by an oral examination.

24. **The sources from which graded-schools may derive their teachers.**—The sources from which graded-schools may receive their best supply of teachers is a question of great practical importance. My own conviction, based on a somewhat extended experience, is that if the system is crowned with a well organized high school, its graduates are likely to make the most successful teachers; and it is from this source that I believe our graded-schools are destined to draw recruits to their teaching force. Teachers who have completed a graded course of instruction which culminates in a well organized high school, have received literary advantages equal to those furnished by any institution below the college or the university. Besides, such teachers will almost invariably be in hearty sympathy with graded-school work. Teachers will teach chiefly as they have been taught, and will manage pupils as they themselves were managed during the course of their education. And if it be true, as I think it is, that the best models of school management are to be found in our well organized

graded-schools, I do not know in what other direction to look for a permanent supply of suitable teachers.

If the reader will keep in mind the distinction which is elsewhere made (§ 9) between the great mass of teachers who know only the art of teaching, and the few who need to know the science of education, it will be seen that provision is made above only for those who are to occupy subordinate positions. The higher professional education of teachers must be acquired in normal schools, or in still higher institutions of learning.

It ought not to be inferred from the above suggestion that it is well to draw all the teachers of a school, or even a large proportion of them, from the school itself. Every school has its peculiar elements of weakness and of strength; and the laws of heredity will work their results here as elsewhere. A repeated involution of peculiarities, such as is inevitable under the circumstances above supposed, will finally result in an abnormal condition of affairs. A school system can not be long maintained in a healthy state without the infusion of new elements.

Some grade of normal instruction should be given in every first-class high school. Large cities should maintain a distinct normal school, whose membership should be composed of high school graduates; while smaller school systems must be content with class instruction in the theory and practice of teaching. Such a class, composed of pupils who propose to teach, reciting twice a week and observing good models, may learn very much about the art of teaching. If such a book as Page's *Theory and Practice of Teaching* be used as a text, to be supplemented and illustrated, teachers may be thoroughly prepared for efficient work in city graded-schools.

Normal instruction given in public schools is justifiable only on the ground that it is necessary for the maintenance of the school system. Considered merely as a preparation for a specific vocation, it is no more within the province of public school work than instruction in medicine or law. The view here taken is, that teachers who have been educated in graded-schools are thereby best qualified for doing graded-school work. If this is not a fact, then the same objection lies against normal instruction as against any other professional instruction.

Universal education at public cost is justifiable only on the ground that it is required for the perpetuity of our civil institutions; and special instruction in any art or trade is justifiable only when the general public good requires it. If it were true that the country in general is suffering from the lack of competent blacksmiths, then it would be a public duty to provide for the training of this class of mechanics.

CHAPTER III.

THE SUPERINTENDENT'S POWERS DEFINED AND SOME OF HIS GENERAL DUTIES DISCUSSED (CONTINUED).

SUMMARY.

The relative fitness of men and women for the management of schools. The use of prescribed books and conformity to the prescribed course of study. The maintenance of discipline. Corporal punishment. Order in the buildings and on the grounds. Recesses. Text-books.

THE SUPERINTENDENT'S POWERS AND DUTIES (CONTINUED).

25. **The relative fitness of men and women for the management of schools.**—Still another question of great practical importance to superintendents and boards of education, is the relative fitness of men and women for the management of schools. This topic is now brought into prominence by its close relation to the general question of the "emancipation of women" which is agitating the public mind. The predominance of women in the school-room is taken as the type of her deserved sphere in all professions; and so the argument takes this form: "Since women are successfully competing with men in the schools, why should they not have the liberty to compete with men everywhere?"

It is a fact that women now greatly outnumber men in the work of the school-room, and the tendency is rapidly toward a monopoly by women of this variety of labor; but still it is a question which at least admits of doubt, whether women are able to do with equal efficiency all the varieties of school work which men are doing. Are there not some portions of this work which women can do much better than men can do them? Are there not other portions which men can do much better than women can do them? Are not the united services of both needed for the highest success of a school system? Analogous questions may be asked which every one can answer; and these answers ought to satisfy all who are in doubt as to woman's legitimate place in the schools. In the training of a family of children, is there not a part of the discipline which can be best administered by the mother? Is there not another part which can be best administered by the father? Are not their united efforts needed for the proper training of the family?

Let it be considered that the first and one of the most difficult duties of the teacher is the discipline of the school, just as the first and one of the most difficult of parental duties is the discipline of the family. The question then at issue is this: Is a woman, as mother or teacher, able to successfully govern children during the successive periods of infancy, childhood, and adolescence? Reasoning from fact, we may learn from the many examples of families left in charge of the mother, that woman, unaided, is not equal to the task of training children in the way they should go; while the known instincts of woman, which prompt her to act from feeling rather than from deliberate purpose, will lead us to expect a weakness in her government of older children. In infancy and early childhood, when weakness demands affection, sympathy, and forbearance, woman is the heaven-appointed disciplinarian; but during the years when the passions exercise their sway, when the will is not controlled by principle, and the strengthened intellect is demanding the right of self-direction, there is need of that judicial firmness which is characteristic of man's nature. Woman is naturally inclined to govern children by persuasion; and when this fails, as it will in multitudes of cases, she will not conquer an unwilling obedience, and so leaves them ungoverned. Persuasion and force, affection uninfluenced by reason, and reason uninfluenced by affection, are the extreme terms of an antithesis which has a real existence in human nature; and it is by reciprocal modifications of these principles that the young are to be trained into habits of obedience.

No; woman can not do man's work in the schools; and one of the greatest dangers which threaten our public school system is the gradual displacement of men from the higher departments, where their influence is especially needed. According to my understanding of the matter, children up to the age of nine years should be instructed and governed almost exclusively by women; from nine to fourteen, they may still be instructed by women, but should be subject, in case of need, to government by men; while from the age of fourteen, they should be taught by both men and women, and should be subject still more to government by men. With respect to instruction, pupils may be taught by women exclusively till the end of the grammar grade; but beyond this there are some branches, as physics, chemistry, and mathematics, which are best taught by men. No one need expect to see a truly prosperous high school in the exclusive charge of women. Two essentials to success will be wanting—healthy discipline and, in some branches, sound instruction. It is just as repugnant to reason and to experience to imagine a high school or college in the exclusive charge of women, as to imagine a primary school in the exclusive charge of men. Each is the climax of absurdity: each is a direct violation of the decrees of nature; for as long as there is sex, there will be characteristic intellectual differences based on sex, and these differences will prescribe spheres of duty which can not be abandoned with impunity.

Since the above was written, my eye has fallen on an extract from the Report of Samuel B. Stone, Superintendent of Schools, Worcester, Mass., which seems to me to embody so much practical wisdom, that I can not forbear to insert it in this connection:

"Nothing is more certain than that the public schools have sadly decreased in effectiveness by forcing from the profession so many of the men. A broad-minded, judicious, and cultivated gentleman is needed at the head of every large school; his influence is as essential to the right formation of character in school as is the father's influence in the proper rearing of a family. Another reason for increasing the number of male teachers is, that a more conservative element—more permanency—may be introduced into the school system among the necessary changes just described. With a competent and permanent head for each school, to preserve the unity, the continuity, and the proper succession of school studies, a teacher may drop out here and there without material loss.

"To secure and retain this increased number of men of this excellence, it would be necessary to pay them liberally, and to secure for the profession a recognized position, such as it hardly holds at present. This *status* of the profession, however, its own members will take care of. The question of salary would involve some additional expense; for men of the right character and ambition for the work they are to do will have families which they must support.

"Right here we are met by the inquiry, Why not increase the pay of your lady teachers, and thus secure them permanently? Because the pay would not hold those whom we most wish to retain, when the trial comes; and because a kind of influence is needed which woman can not exert. Do what she will, try as she may, no true woman can so obliterate the mental and spiritual, any more than the physical marks by which the Creator has distinguished and glorified her, as to act to perfection the man. The thousand little differences of character which display themselves in male and female teachers are fully recognized by all except the few who, in laboring for what they call the elevation of woman, think it necessary to establish her identity with man, in order to disprove her inferiority.

"What we need is more of strong manly character in our schools; and to secure this we must attract it from other callings. As for having the work done as well by women, there is a part which she can do far better, a part equally well, and a part not at all. Her superiority in educating little children, when the heart is in the work, can not be denied; her equality in the work of instruction is plain; but drill is not all of school. In the development of character, the influence of woman is indispensable; but she alone would make boys womanish and girls not altogether womanly.

"There is an exciting question about paying a woman the same salary as a man for the same work! No one will deny the justice of this demand. The work needed, and for which I am contending, is what she can not do. There is, therefore, no competition. There is, moreover, a law of supply and demand which regulates prices; they can not be regulated by legislative enactments. The price of wheat can not be fixed by statute. If an educated woman is wanted to fill a certain position, and ten stand ready to take it at $1,000, each fully competent, is there any propriety in paying $2,000? Will that help the nine? If an educated man is wanted for a position at $2,000, which a man only can fill, and a suitable man can not be secured for less than $2,500, will it be best to take one of the nine women? At any rate, this is what we have been doing thirty or forty years, and, as many persons best qualified to judge think, with injury to the schools.

"Is there any reason in the constitution of society why

there should be ten women for the one place and not the right man for the other? There are indisputable indications that men and women are in all respects the counterparts of each other. The Creator did not fall into an error when he made woman, as certain modern reformers would seem to imply. In all civil society, since there was a civil society, man has been regarded as the bread-winner and woman the house-keeper. Probably this is about right, since a great deal of homely joy has resulted. A young man who rightly expects in the main to carry out this idea, will not and ought not to enter a profession without promise. On the other hand, there is a large class of self-dependent women. The majority of those who teach are young. Many, with true heroism, labor and secure for themselves not only a livelihood, but the means of improvement, and a culture and refinement that ought to be the envy of indolent ladies of wealth. These heroic women are worthy of all honor, but should they be treated as the rule or the exception? Should laws and customs be changed as if all women were to take such places?

"This question of employment and salaries for women is deeper than the surface. The present order of things, in this regard, has its foundation in the very organization of society. That order, with all its defects, should not be rudely changed at the risk of greater evils.

"In what has thus far been said, I wish to be distinctly understood as not undervaluing the services of women in the schools. In all which is common between male and female teachers, I can match the best man with an equally excellent woman; while in that which belongs to woman only, she is the superior. The influence of man, now too feebly felt in the schools, is what is here contended for. If the proportion of male and female teachers were reversed, this whole argument would apply to the other side; but as it is, the one thing needful for our public schools is to add permanently to the corps of teachers twice the number of men, and only those of the better class."

26. **The use of prescribed books and conformity to the prescribed course of study.** — All organized bodies are threatened with the danger of disintegration, and the highest forms of organization are most exposed to disintegrating forces. In graded-schools, the tendency to disorganization is felt in the unwillingness of pupils to conform to the requirements of classification. This protest against conformity to the established order of things may manifest itself in unwillingness to use prescribed text-books, or to pursue the appointed studies of the course. Even now it is not quite clear to all parents why their children may not be allowed to use whatever books it suits their convenience to furnish; and to many it appears like an arbitrary act to refuse a free choice in the selection of studies. Nonconformity in either case, however, can not be tolerated without great danger to the system; and ceaseless vigilance should be exercised against the encroachments of this evil. Two things should be absolutely forbidden: the use of any text-book not in the prescribed list, and the study of any subject not included in the prescribed course. To allow either of these things to be done is to sanction the gradual disorganization of a graded-school.

But it does not follow from these prohibitions that every pupil must necessarily pursue all the studies which are prescribed for a given grade. The organization of the school — the prescribed number and sequence of studies — may remain intact, even if some pupils pursue only a part of the course. Disorganization will set in only when no one chooses to pursue a given study of the course. In this case, the continuity of the course will be broken, and the first downward step will be taken toward an ungraded school. The greatest good of pupils in general, and the highest prosperity of the school,—two things which are inseparable even in thought,—both require a close conformity to the prescribed course of instruction; but there are cases in which exceptions may be made to this general rule with advantage to individual pupils and without harm to the general system. Pupils may be excused from certain studies of the course under the following circumstances:

(1) When a pupil's health will not permit him to take the full course, and there is the alternative of taking a part of it or of leaving school altogether.

(2) When a pupil can spend but a short time in school, and has good reasons for bestowing all his attention on two or three selected studies.

When these exceptions are made, it should be with the distinct understanding that the pupils who avail themselves of them are disqualified for promotion. It is plain that one part of a graded course must be completed before a succeeding part can be attempted. This check is absolutely required in order to preserve the integrity of the system, and will be found sufficient to prevent any unnecessary exceptions to the general rule.

27. The maintenance of discipline.—The strength, or it may be the weakness, of a superintendent or of a principal, is nowhere so clearly shown as in the general discipline of the school. Individual teachers, in cases of extreme difficulty which will occur at intervals, must of necessity rely on their superior for the enforcement of obedience. At any rate, the head of a school must take some stand in this matter, since pupils or their parents will certainly appeal to him, on occasion, for a redress of wrongs real or imagined.

Teachers will secure that degree of discipline which they are sustained in enforcing, or which they are required to enforce; and any weakness, indecision, or vacillation in the superintendent will immediately show its effects in the school.

For the maintenance of healthy discipline, it is not necessary that there should be great severity in the punishment of offenses. The absolute certainty that the teacher's authority will be upheld, and that, in case of need, the supreme authority in the school will be invoked, is, in most cases, sufficient in itself to hold the evil propensities of pupils in check. On the contrary, a want of firmness will encourage the spirit of revolt, and make necessary a frequent resort to punishments of one kind or another.

The sense of justice is strong even in the case of vicious children. They know that disobedience and wrong-doing in general deserve punishment; and, provided the good intent of the disciplinarian is manifest, and the degree of punishment does not exceed its just bounds, no feeling of resentment will be cherished toward him who inflicts the penalty. While children soon learn to feel a contempt for a superior who does not insist on respectful obedience, they instinctively admire that manly energy of character which metes out to offenders their deserved punishment. If, however, pupils are punished in anger or beyond measure, it is probable that evil and not good will be done.

Every effort should be made to convince pupils that they will encounter the consequences of their own wrong-doing; that if trouble must come, they, and not their superiors, will be responsible for it. To this end it is often best to defer a punishment, giving the offender chance to mend his ways. In this case there is danger, of course, that the pupil may presume on such forbearance, and feel encouraged to persevere in his evil ways; but the remedy for this is the well-known firmness of the authority which can afford to wait, but which is neither forgetful nor neglectful.

In what has preceded it is tacitly assumed that there are occasions in which corporal punishment is necessary, and therefore justifiable. While I am conscious that many judicious educators discard this manner of discipline, I am free to express my conviction that it is sometimes the teacher's only available resource to secure to the school and to the offender their respective rights. A school must be preserved from disorder and from the contagion of bad examples; and there is no more sacred duty binding on parents and teachers than to require of children prompt and respectful obedience. Children should be exhorted and encouraged in every proper manner to do right, because the doing of right is in itself a comely and virtuous thing; but when exhortation, expostulation, and admonition have no effect, what is to be done? Manifestly, that degree of force should be employed which will conquer obedience. All will allow that a cheerful, voluntary obedience is the truly desirable thing; but is not an enforced obedience to be preferred to disobedience?

Government is positive, not negative; it does not consist in advising people what to do, leaving the matter, in the end, to their own discretion. It assumes that some will choose to do what ought not to be done, and so places before them a penalty sufficient to secure an enforced obedience. In the absence of internal motives to do right, the law holds forth an artificial motive in the form of a penalty attached to violations of prescribed laws.

28. **Corporal punishment.** — As a last resort, therefore, force is justifiable. Now force, when actually brought to bear on an offender, resolves itself into some bodily affection. There is either some restraint put upon the usual

bodily activities, or, proceeding to extremities, there is an infliction of bodily pain. This last constitutes corporal punishment as generally understood. If, then, it is allowed that obedience is necessary, it will take place under some one of the following cases:

(1) Spontaneously — without any traceable suggestion — by the unconscious promptings of one's moral nature.

(2) By suggestion, advice, admonition, or warning.

(3) By some restraint on personal liberties.

(4) By the infliction of bodily pain.

Up to this point it is scarcely conceivable that there is real ground for difference of opinion; but when the subject is considered with special reference to public school policy, two theories may be maintained:

(*a*) An observance of the rules and regulations shall be a condition of school membership; and when obedience is not rendered as under cases (1) and (2), the offender is to be suspended from school.

(*b*) One of the objects of public school training is to inculcate the habit of obedience and a respect for authority; and to this end, in cases where obedience is not rendered as above, teachers may restrain the liberties of pupils; or, if this does not suffice, they may resort to the extreme measure of inflicting pain.

There is no doubt that all teachers would prefer to work under the first plan: it would make the task of governing infinitely easy. In fact, there would be no such thing as school government, in the proper sense of the term; for whenever pupils did not yield a voluntary obedience, they would cease to require any positive direction by the teacher. But it is quite as certain that most parents wish to place upon the teachers of their children the task of securing obedience, even at the expense of inflicting needed corporal punishment. In general, there is nothing against which parents more heartily protest than the trouble and vexation of correcting children for offenses committed in school. "Have they not enough to do to attend to the correction of their children for home faults? Should not teachers be competent to govern their pupils? What fitness have they for their office, if they can not enforce obedience when occasion requires?"

This is the current theory held by parents; and until there is a decided change in public sentiment, I do not see how the schools can renounce the duty of securing obedience even at the expense of corporal punishment. Teachers would most gladly be relieved from such a disagreeable task. It is not from any fondness for the punishing of pupils that they persist in it, but because they believe it to be a duty imposed on them by the public whose servants they are. But they may rightly demand at least a partial release from this most ungrateful duty. In cases where pupils persist in wrong-doing, uninfluenced by mild measures, parents should be asked to choose between correcting their children themselves and submitting them to such discipline as the teacher may judge necessary. Two good results would come from this course: responsibility for the bad conduct of children would be placed where it in great part belongs, and school authorities would be shielded from any imputation of needlessly resorting to corporal punishment.

Is it not possible that those who are so radically opposed to corporal punishment make the mistake of looking on human nature as it ought to be, and not as it actually is? Most children are not in that moral condition in which good conduct is determined by the unconscious impulses of a noble nature; and but very few teachers have reached that degree of perfection whereby they can govern pupils by "moral suasion" alone. It is true that the best teachers have least occasion to employ force; perhaps it is true that teachers are good just in proportion as they can govern by tact, sympathy, or affection; but it does not follow from this that the more imperfect modes of discipline should be abandoned. If teachers are required to secure obedience, they should do it by the mildest means at their command; but they must do it at all hazards. Here, as elsewhere, human imperfection must be recognized as a fact; and while we are required to do a certain work, we must be allowed to use our own tools, even though they are imperfect. In other words, it is better that a school should be governed by harsh methods than not be governed at all.

As a general rule, children who are well governed at home occasion no trouble in school; while most of the "incorrigibles" who vex teachers' souls are the product of parental mismanagement. There is but little hope, therefore, that any reform will be worked in such cases by remanding offenders to home discipline. By reason of the strong and almost inexplicable influence which is exercised by numbers, it sometimes happens that children who are models of propriety at home are tempted into bad conduct in school. Such cases, in general, can be cured by coöperating with the home authorities; and if all cases of discipline were of this class, the rod might be banished from the school-room.

29. Order in the buildings and on the grounds.— As the teacher is required to maintain good order in the school room, so the superintendent or principal must secure the orderly movements of the pupils throughout the building and on the grounds; and the general appearance of a school while pupils are entering or leaving a house is a very fair indication of the managing ability of the responsible head. If the stairways are broad and straight, there need be no serious difficulty in maintaining good order; but if, as is too often the case, they are narrow and crooked, the difficulties are greatly increased. Halls and stairways may be so constructed that pupils can be seen by their teachers during almost the entire march up and down; but it is often the case that they are out of sight after the first few steps; and under such circumstances, means must be taken to secure a strict oversight of the halls by the teachers in general.

An observance of the following rules will contribute very largely to the maintenance of good order in passing to and from the rooms:

(1) Definite times of dismission should be arranged, so that the several schools may not interfere with one another while going out. Thus, the schools on the first floor should be dismissed first, and their relative times of dismission should be so arranged that all interference may be avoided.

(2) If there are stairways both in front and in rear, certain schools should invariably have their exit by the first and the others as invariably by the second.

(3) If the stairways are wide, boys should invariably pass down by one railing and girls by the other; but if they are narrow, the boys should pass down first and then the girls.

(4) Preparatory to passing down, pupils should be arranged in the halls in single file, and at a given signal the column should move.

(5) Pupils should invariably walk while moving up and down or through the halls, and all talking and whispering should be avoided.

(6) When pupils enter the building, they should follow the same route as in going down, and should proceed directly to their rooms.

(7) When pupils pass from the building, they should leave the premises at once; they should not be allowed to wait on the steps or at the gates.

30. Recesses.—In crowded city schools, where playgrounds are limited to a few rods of bare earth, many evils are connected with the usual forenoon and afternoon recesses. In general, the promiscuous mingling of such large numbers of children of both sexes is liable to the gravest objections. The sport is violent and boisterous, involving frequent quarrels, and entailing disorder of every variety and degree. That which takes place is not healthful recreation; and the presence of so much that is rough and uncouth has a most unfavorable influence on morals and manners. We have not to do with quiet recreations on ample grass-plots, which children in isolated schools may enjoy, but with the pell-mell and hurly-burly which are unavoidable when hundreds of pupils are thrown together in the smaller yards connected with city schools. In such cases I believe the usual recesses are prolific sources of evil, and that their direct tendency is to vitiate our public school system.

Some who have felt the magnitude of this evil have made trial of a plan which is free from many of the objections which have been mentioned. It is still an experiment, and must submit to the ordeal of experience, which is the final test of all our methods. It is an innovation on the established order of things, and, as such, will be charged with evils which do not belong to it. Doubtless it will be found objectionable in some points; but if it is found to reduce the acknowledged evils of the present system to their minimum, without entailing others of grave character, it is worthy of a careful trial. This plan is as follows: the sessions open at 9 A. M. and at 1–30 P. M., respectively, and close at 11 A. M. and at 3 P. M. for the lower grades, and thirty minutes later for the higher grades. The usual recesses are abolished. Pupils are excused from the room, one or two at a time, while classes are changing, on condition of remaining for a stated time after the close of the session. Pupils whose state of health demands a freedom from ordinary restraint are excused without exacting a penalty. This exception is made only when teachers have positive assurance that physical weakness requires it. The check placed on leave of absence should be just sufficient to prevent fictitious excuses.

With judicious teachers who are good disciplinarians, this plan is not subject to any grave objections. It may be urged, at first sight, that by this plan children are kept in close confinement too long; but when it is recollected that pupils are alternately reciting and studying, and consequently in motion to a considerable extent, and that proper precaution will secure a frequent change of air, it will appear that this objection is imaginary rather than real. Finally, it may be remarked that, after trying this system for several years, and being ready to abandon it at any moment should it prove decidedly objectionable, I have every reason to believe that it is an improvement on the system which has been consecrated by immemorial use.

31. Text-books.—Next to the teacher, the text-book stands in closest relation to the prosperity of a school. As a summary of facts and principles skillfully classified and fit to be committed to memory, and thus to transmit the acquired knowledge of one generation to the next, its importance in the work of instruction can not be overestimated. The text-book is to the school what machinery is to a complex industrial process. In each case the quality of the work done depends very largely on the perfection of the tools which are employed.

Changes in school-books are often the occasion of disturbance, and it is of great importance to settle on some principles which shall be observed in their introduction.

Clearly, the superintendent has no right whatever to introduce a text-book on his own authority; but it is equally true that in a matter of this nature his judgment and wishes should be consulted. No one is in so good a position to judge of the fitness of a text-book as the superintendent. Familiar with the general scheme of instruction, and knowing the requirements of the several grades, he should be able to form a trustworthy judgment as to the quality and the quantity of matter needed in each department of the school. Competence in this direction is, indeed, a professional duty, just as it is a professional duty for a surgeon to select the instruments which are needed in his practice. But as the absolute quality of text-books is not the only question at stake, as there may be circumstances which would render the adoption of even an improved book inopportune, and as the Board is best able to judge of these incidental elements, it is plain that the Board must be the final judge in the case, and should, if thought necessary, set aside an opinion based on intrinsic merit.

Changes in text-books are sometimes made without due consideration. Books in use are sometimes thrown out without sufficient cause, and new ones are introduced without particular reference to fitness. It should be a fixed principle with the Board to consider such subjects with deliberation and make only such changes as are demanded to promote the best interests of the schools.

The prosperity of American schools is due in great measure to the enterprise and liberality of American publishers, who have fostered and almost created the authorship of text-books which are a credit to our age and country; for it is a fact beyond dispute that the American school-book has no superior. No class of books is subject to such rigorous and decisive criticism as this; and no other branch of trade responds so promptly to the interests and wants of the public. Competition drives poor books from the market.

While a conservative policy is the one to be generally pursued, there are occasions when a change in text-books may be made with propriety. Changes are justifiable on the following grounds:

(1) When the new book is manifestly superior to the old in the quality of its matter and in systematic arrangement.

(2) When a book in use does not represent the actual state of the science, by reason of new and important discoveries made since its publication.

(3) When the successful working of the graded course of instruction requires an increase or a diminution in the quantity of matter.

With reference to these items it is to be remarked that there is a real difference in the quality of books. It is not true, as some pretend, that all recent books on a specified subject are equally meritorious, and may therefore be used with equal advantage. There are the same differences in text-books as in other literary productions; and their use will meet with corresponding success. Some books are intrinsically excellent, and others intrinsically bad; and between these extremes there are all shades of quality. It is sometimes said, in reply to this, that a good teacher should be able to give instruction from any text-book, or even without one. This is in a measure true; but as it is a fact that pupils are required to derive the greater part of their information from books, it is a matter of the highest importance that they be properly written.

Again, a book may be unfit for use because it has become

antiquated. This may happen in the case of the sciences which are growing rapidly, such as Physiology, Geography, Geology, and Chemistry. A text-book on either of these sciences may represent the existing state of knowledge to-day, but the discoveries of another year may make them more or less obsolete. The boundaries of human knowledge are ever enlarging, and new facts may give a new interpretation to well-known phenomena. Changes of this nature should be incorporated into our educational literature in order that the schools may fulfill their legitimate purpose. We are quick to change the style of our dress on the appearance of a mere change in the *mode;* yet we feel impelled to say harsh things when asked to substitute a modern text-book for one which is antiquated, and is therefore an incumbrance.

Finally, the exigencies of a graded course of instruction may require the substitution of one book for another. This may happen when a change in the grading has been made, or when the natural working of the system has shown that a book is inadequate to the demands made on it. Instances have occurred in which a course of instruction has been drawn up with a more direct reference to series of Geographies, Arithmetics, and Grammars, which must needs be used, than to the probable duration of the child's school-life. In such cases, when the course of instruction has been reduced to reasonable limits, a corresponding change in text-books is required.

When, for valid reasons, a change in text-books has been ordered, it is frequently most expedient to replace the old ones by a process of gradual substitution. When beginning classes are formed, pupils should be instructed to buy the new book instead of the old one. In this way most of the objections to a change in books may be avoided.

If books are introduced, it should be through the regular channels of trade. Neither superintendent nor teachers should, under any ordinary circumstances, supply pupils with any merchandise used in school. Booksellers sometimes suffer loss from unsalable stock, left on their hands by a change in text-books, and they are at all times entitled to whatever profits arise from this branch of trade. Even when school authorities sell books to pupils without hope of gain, they are liable to unjust suspicion.

CHAPTER IV.

THE SUPERINTENDENT'S POWERS DEFINED AND SOME OF HIS GENERAL DUTIES DISCUSSED (CONCLUDED).

SUMMARY.

The relation of the superintendent to subordinate teachers. The independence of teachers. Form of superintendent's record. The assistance which should be rendered to teachers. The dismission of teachers. The granting of testimonials. The considerate treatment of teachers. Teachers' meetings. To what extent a teacher's acts should be sanctioned.

THE SUPERINTENDENT'S POWERS AND DUTIES (CONCLUDED).

32. The relation of the superintendent to subordinate teachers.—As already indicated, there must be some definite relation between the responsible head of a school and his subordinates. Unity and harmony can be maintained only by carrying into effect the general plans and necessary orders which proceed from a recognized authority. In the absence of some well defined motives for conforming to the prescribed order of things, some degree of insubordination is likely to occur. A school in which factions exist can be saved from ruin only by the prompt exercise of authority; and unless there is a well-grounded feeling that the positions which teachers hold depend somewhat on the will of the person in charge, there will not be a hearty coöperation and a cheerful compliance with what is required. It is, perhaps, to be regretted that such motives as these should be necessary; but in this case, as in all of a like nature, things must be considered as they are, and not merely as they ought to be. Whether teachers shall be employed or not should depend, to a considerable extent, on the superintendent's opinion of their fidelity to duty, and the real success which they have accomplished. Were positions independent of desert, those who hold them would feel but little zeal in their allotted work.

It is not to be inferred from this that differences in opinion are not to be tolerated. Obsequiousness is more to be suspected than firmness in holding to one's opinions. It is not necessary that teachers echo all the opinions of their superior. It is rather an evidence of extreme weakness. Independent thought is compatible with the most hearty loyalty, and is a trait of character to be respected and cherished. Where there is healthy intellectual activity, there will be differences of opinion; but these need not interfere with the duty of obedience. Some minds take great delight in mere uniformities. It might be a beautiful uniformity if all who live in the same longitude were to rise at the same moment each morning; but it would be a very absurd thing nevertheless.

33. **The independence of teachers.**—To what extent should the superintendent interfere with teachers in their work? The general principle is easily stated. Teachers are to be held responsible for the quality of their instruction and discipline, and should be allowed to follow their own methods so far as is consistent with general requirements. The seating of pupils, their manner of coming to the place of recitation; special means of securing order in the room, and other items of similar character should be entrusted to the teacher's judgment. Within her room, the teacher should be mistress of the situation; and only under extraordinary circumstances has the superintendent a right to make direct interference. The individual rights of the teacher should be as clearly recognized as those of the superintendent or of the Board. Good teachers will do more work, and of better quality, if confidence is reposed in their judgment and discretion. The superintendent is in duty bound to proffer suggestions and advice when they are known to be needed; but in many cases it is best to go no further.

Where there is no violation of established principles, it is well to allow considerable latitude of judgment, and to wait for results before making direct interference. Teachers are not to be transformed into mere *automata*, but are to be credited with good intentions, and helped to become efficient co-laborers, while retaining all proper freedom of thought and action. Perpetual interference in minor matters, which will usually work their own cure, is a capital fault in school management. A school should be a republic, not a despotism; an organic whole, animated by self-active centers, not a dead machine, kept in motion by external force. Hold teachers responsible for results, aid them by suggestion and advice, and allow them all possible freedom in developing their plans and methods.

The same principle should be observed in assisting teachers as in assisting pupils. Indirect help is best. They are most truly aided who are put in the way of aiding themselves. In the case of teachers, this principle is of peculiar importance. A teacher's methods should have a large element of personality in them — they can not be copied bodily from others. The uniformities which are desirable are typical merely. There should be a general resemblance in methods for a special purpose; but it is not necessary, nor even desirable, that they be exact copies of one another. Growths which are in any sense vital, have an individual character; they are founded on a common type, but are distinguished by unimportant differences. In methods of teaching and discipline, typical uniformities alone are desirable.

34. **Form of superintendent's record.** — A superintendent will form a just estimate of a teacher's ability by directing his attention systematically to a few points of chief importance. Ability to keep order, power of holding attention, knowledge of the subject, skill in imparting instruction,

are qualifications which should enter as elements into the superintendent's judgment of a teacher's worth. It is a good plan to make a record of each teacher's ability in these particulars. The opposite blank is presented as a specimen page of a SUPERINTENDENT'S REGISTER, to be used for the purpose above mentioned. After a succession of visits, an average of all the marks will represent the superintendent's estimate of each teacher's ability. This plan has evident advantages. (1) It gives system and exactness to the work of supervision. A school is visited with the express purpose of testing the teacher's efficiency in certain material points. (2) In case teachers know what excellencies are expected, or from what data an estimate of their success will be formed, they, too, will have a definite purpose in the performance of their work. (3) Whenever it is necessary to inform the Board of a teacher's qualifications, a trustworthy statement can be made.

35. **The assistance which should be rendered to teachers.**—Whenever it is seen that a teacher is making a radical mistake which will compromise her success, a full and frank statement of the fact is required, and such helps should be given as the case seems to demand. No false delicacy should tempt one to withhold a candid opinion as to the nature and consequences of glaring faults. Otherwise, when disaster has come, and the teacher has forfeited her place, there is just ground for charging the superintendent with neglect of duty; for it is plain that skillful supervision ought to diminish the chances of failure. The superintendent ought to be a teacher of teachers, competent to detect the probable causes of failure, and able to suggest means which may avert disaster. This course is of special importance in the case of inexperienced teachers, whom judicious criticism and skillful assistance may save from undeserved failure.

SUPERINTENDENT'S REGISTER.

NAMES OF TEACHERS.	ORDER.	POWER OF HOLDING ATTENTION.	SKILL IN INSTRUCTION.	SKILL IN DISCIPLINE.	MANNER.	GENERAL IMPRESSION.	AVERAGE STANDING.
Miss F. A.	9	8	7	8	8	8	$8\frac{1}{3}$
	9	9	8	8	9	9	
Miss B. M.	7	7	6	7	7	6	$7\frac{3}{4}$
	8	8	8	7	8	8	
Miss A. C.	10	9	8	8	7	8	$8\frac{1}{2}$
	9	9	8	9	8	9	

In too many instances teachers are allowed to fail. The danger is seen, but no warning is given, no advice proffered; when, suddenly, the teacher is overwhelmed with failure, and can not resist the feeling that she has been unfaithfully treated. Great good often comes from allowing teachers to exchange visits. In this way individual excellencies become common property, and faults, seen in others, become noticeable and are shunned.

36. **The dismission of teachers.**—But after all the helps which a wise supervision can render, teachers may fail to do satisfactory work; and it is often a question of extreme delicacy and difficulty to decide when a teacher should be displaced. On one side are the teacher's interests, her reputation, the mortification of failure; and, on the other, the interests of the school. From similarity of position, the sympathies of the superintendent will naturally incline to the side of the teacher; while, as a public servant, obliged by the very nature of his office to protect the rights of the people as represented in their children, he can not allow a school to suffer from the incompetence of its teachers. It is necessary to recollect that a school is not a benevolent institution for giving aid to needy teachers. The needs of the school must be considered first; and if it appears that it is retrograding in point of discipline or scholarship, there should be no hesitation in recommending a change. In this situation of affairs, the danger seldom lies in the direction of hasty action, but rather in that of putting off the evil day, hoping for amendment and a triumph over difficulties, particularly in the case of a teacher who is putting forth every effort to succeed.

When the Board has decided that dismission is necessary, this duty, though an unpleasant one, should be performed in an honorable manner. The teacher should be told plainly, but kindly, the necessities of the case; there should be no deception, no double-dealing. The instances are too frequent in which moral cowardice has added unnecessary pangs to misfortune. The notice of dismission, instead of being given at the earliest practicable day, has sometimes followed the teacher on her vacation visit to a distant home.

37. **The granting of testimonials.**—When teachers have thus forfeited their places through incompetence, what are their rights as to testimonials and recommendations? There is a practice too general, and attended by many evil consequences, of granting even to grossly incompetent teachers flattering recommendations. The practical result of this has been to throw deserved and almost universal discredit on testimonials from school officers. It must be allowed that it is often very difficult to decide what equal and exact justice requires. Often there is the possibility, even the probability, that under different circumstances, under the stimulus of a new effort, a different result might be reached; and in such cases it seems unjust to stand in the way of an opportunity to vindicate one's self. The usual practice of school officers is either to grant a flattering commendation, or to draw up a document in ambiguous terms, giving prominence to exceptional excellencies, and keeping silence as to well-known faults. There is but one general rule to be followed: either refuse to grant such papers or tell the whole truth. For the common good, something should be done to redeem testimonials from the almost universal contempt into which they have so justly fallen.

38. **The considerate treatment of teachers.**—Every legitimate means should be used to render the situation of teachers agreeable and comfortable. At best, they are ex-

posed to many annoyances incident to their calling, and it is cruel to add others which are avoidable. Teachers should not be treated as the mere hirelings of a day, liable to be displaced without warning; but they should feel assured that their positions are safe as long as they render efficient service. Teachers who have earned a right to confidence should be employed at least by the year; they should be spared the anxieties and uncertainties which attend frequent reëlections. When long service has given positive assurance of merit, why should it be thought necessary to limit the reëngagement to a single term?

Teachers should be paid promptly at the close of each month. Their salaries are usually meager, but little more than sufficient to pay current expenses, and it is a cruelty scarcely pardonable to delay the payment of what is needed for almost daily necessities.

39. **Teachers' Meetings.**—The theory of school supervision which this treatise is designed to illustrate requires the superintendent to work upon the school through the teachers. He is to prepare plans of instruction and discipline, which the teachers must carry into effect; but the successful working out of such a scheme requires constant oversight and constant readjustments. Hence arises the necessity for conference, instruction in methods, and correction of errors. The teachers of a graded-school should be under continual normal instruction. At stated periods, meetings should be held for instruction in all departments of practical school work; and to this there should be added, as occasion admits, instruction in the principles which underlie successful practice, to the end that teachers may become intelligent and independent co-laborers. (§ 9.)

Teachers' Meetings are the only known means of giving harmony and proper efficiency to a system of instruction.

That unity of purpose and of method, which is indispensable to success, can not be communicated in any other manner; nor is there any other way of giving due prominence to that *esprit de corps* which should animate a body of teachers.

The frequency of these meetings should be regulated by the circumstances of the school. Under a new administration there will be need to call teachers together frequently, especially if affairs are to take a new direction, — if a new policy is to be inaugurated; and if there are many changes in teachers, there is need of frequent conference for instruction and advice. Under such circumstances, two meetings each month are desirable. When a school has been brought into general conformity to a settled line of policy, and when there are only occasional breaks in the ranks of teachers, monthly meetings will suffice. And if, as is very proper, this meeting is made the occasion to pay the month's salary, teachers will attend cheerfully and promptly. Except in large cities, where teachers are scattered over a wide area, these meetings are most conveniently held on Fridays, at the close of the afternoon session.

It is probable that the superintendent, in his round of visits, has noticed errors which are more or less common. These should be brought to the attention of the whole body of teachers; the exact nature of the faults should be pointed out, and appropriate remedies suggested. This correction of errors will form a very important part of the business which may appropriately come before a teachers' meeting. It scarcely requires to be added that these criticisms should be impersonal, and should be made in the utmost kindness, and with the sole purpose of promoting the general good. Another very important order of business is instruction in methods of teaching and discipline. The superintendent, by virtue of his office, should be able to give professional instruction of this kind. He should take up one topic after another, in the order of its importance, and should discuss it philosophically; that is, disclose the principles which underlie the methods under consideration. If grammar is indifferently taught, this subject should be discussed in such a way as to make apparent the cause of the difficulty; and a system of instruction should be marked out, designed to inaugurate a better order of things.

It will often be found useful to call special meetings of the teachers interested in the same topic. For example, if there is need of giving more attention to geography, the teachers of this subject should be called together for special instruction. If there is a weak point in any part of the system, it should be strengthened by a concentration of attention upon that definite object. A policy of this kind, patiently carried forward, will soon reinvigorate the whole system.

40. To what extent a teacher's acts should be sanctioned.—With respect to discipline, it is important to know to what extent a superintendent is justifiable in sanctioning the measures which teachers may think best to employ. On the one hand, individual teachers can not maintain efficient discipline without the moral and sometimes the physical support of their superiors; and, on the other, no sane man is willing to pledge himself, in advance, to sanction all that inexperienced or injudicious teachers may occasionally do.

When teachers have followed the plain line of duty, and particularly when they have carried out instructions, and have fallen into trouble in consequence, it is poltroonery to desert them in their extremity. Even when teachers have been somewhat injudicious under trying circumstances, when there was no opportunity for deliberation, they should be supported so far as is consistent with truthfulness and honor, if it is evident that their general course has been directed by fidelity to duty.

On the contrary, when teachers go counter to instructions, or when they adopt methods of discipline which are open to grave objection, or inflict punishment which is grossly excessive, they should be allowed to suffer the natural consequences of their folly. In such cases, when parents remonstrate, as they ought to do, the acts complained of should be disavowed, and all proper reparation made. While no general rule can be given which will anticipate specific cases, a correct sense of justice will usually dictate the course which should be followed.

CHAPTER V.

THE ART OF GRADING SCHOOLS.

SUMMARY.

Graded-school defined. The advantages of graded-schools. Schools should conform to the needs and circumstances of communities. Ideal of a graded-school. Data to be used in grading. Limitations of data. Can country schools be graded? The grading of a small school illustrated. The arrangement of text-book work. The arrangement of programmes. The development of a provisional classification. The successive transformations through which a graded-school may pass. Synopsis of a common school course of instruction.

THE ART OF GRADING SCHOOLS.

41. **Graded-School defined.**—A school in which pupils are classified according to their attainments, and in which pupils of similar attainments are taught together, and thus pursue the successive portions of a systematic course of instruction, is a Graded-School. If the course covers a period of twelve years, each year's work may constitute a grade; and when pupils have completed a year's work in a satisfactory manner, they are promoted to the next higher grade. In other cases, the whole course of instruction is divided into a smaller number of periods, each of which is called a grade or department. Thus the twelve years of school life may be distinguished into three periods as follows: A primary grade or department of four years, a grammar grade of four years, and a high school grade of four years. The essential idea is to subdivide the work of instruction into a series of ascending steps, each of which is preparatory to the next in succession.

42. **The advantages of graded-schools.**—The advantages of such a system are obvious.

(1) It is an application to the work of instruction of the great law of the division of labor. By this means a teacher's time, talent, and attention are concentrated on a prescribed range of duties, which become easy by repetition, and hence

are likely to be performed in a thorough manner. Advantage is also taken of the fitness of teachers for special varieties of work. Some teachers are most skillful in teaching children, others in teaching adults; some who would succeed but indifferently in one grade, may be eminently successful in another.

(2) Pupils who pursue their studies under such a system derive peculiar advantages from the thoroughness of their instruction, and the completeness of the course; for not only is a reasonable degree of proficiency in the studies of one grade necessary for promotion to a higher, but there is no *hiatus* in the course of instruction.

The work of teaching thus follows the law which prevails in all well-regulated industries. This general movement is characteristic of a growing civilization, and it is as reasonable to cry out against the division of labor in general as against that special application of the law which has called into being the Graded-School.

43. Schools should conform to the needs and circumstances of communities. — Perhaps the most difficult task in practical school work is to arrange a course of instruction which is best adapted to given circumstances. Two important considerations should not be overlooked:

(1) Every graded system should be somewhat elastic — should afford opportunities for growth and for the readjustments which a gradual development of the system may require, or which the general educational current of the day may make necessary. The working, for several years, of a course which has been very nicely adjusted, will almost unavoidably disclose the need of some modification; and the changes which are gradually taking place in public opinion on educational topics ought to have their effect on practical education. Organization should promote growth,

not arrest it. There should be enough elasticity in the structure to allow the organism to respond insensibly to the impulses of growth; there should not be that rigidity which checks expansion till the imprisoned forces assert their supremacy with violence.

(2) Graded systems of instruction should adapt themselves to the needs and circumstances of communities. The ideal element—the consideration of what ought to be, should enter into the structure of every system; but no less imperative is the need of keeping the mind intent on the actual state of the people whose interests are to be promoted. For the schools belong to the people; and the opinions, interests, and, to some extent, even the whims of the people must be respected. It is not meant by this that the schools are to react to every suggestion, wise or foolish, friendly or sinister, which may come from without, for it is to shield them from such calamities that Boards of Trustees interfere between these organizations and the caprices of individual opinion; but it is meant that no institution which draws its support from the people at large can safely disregard the candid suggestions of public opinion. Now, it is conceivable that two towns of equal school population, but of different material resources, intellectual tastes, and degrees of culture, may require systems of public instruction which are somewhat different; while it is plain that towns whose populations differ considerably in size, require marked differences in courses of study. Here has been a fundamental and most mischievous error, especially in the organization of high schools. Small towns, with scant materials for a high school, frequently adopt courses of study which only the resources of the larger cities can carry into effect. For the sake of *eclat*, an expense is incurred wholly out of proportion to the interests involved. Two or three pupils in

Latin, Greek, or Trigonometry sometimes monopolize time which should be given to larger classes in more practical studies. If the principal be a mathematician, he is in danger of drawing up a course of mathematics, fit only for a college; and other tastes here find a field for their display. He who thus allows individual preferences to govern him, is incapable of arranging a course of study for the average pupil.

44. **Ideal of a graded-school.**—Preparatory to the object we have in view, it is necessary to form a clear notion of the requirements of a perfectly graded school. The essential idea, as the term grade itself suggests, is that of an orderly succession of ascending steps, each of which is a necessary preparation for the one which follows. Each of these steps consists in a competent knowledge of three or four subjects of instruction; and when a pupil has passed a satisfactory examination in each of the topics which constitute one grade, he is promoted to the next higher grade, where he will continue the studies of the lower grade, or will take others which follow in natural order. Let the reader imagine a large school-room, containing three successive series of ascending steps, representing the three grades into which the course of instruction is divided. These are named the primary grade, the grammar grade, and the high school grade. The primary and grammar grades constitute what is called the common school course; and the high school grade, the secondary course. Each grade is subdivided into four shorter steps, each of which occupies one year of study.

Let us suppose that the pupils in this school have been pursuing their studies for one year, and that the pupils seated in each subdivision are to take one step in advance The highest class in the high school will pass out of the room, and a new class will enter from without and take the places vacated by the lowest class in the primary grade. If, for any reason, certain pupils have not done the work prescribed for them, they will remain behind and mingle with the class which has come forward. And if, during the year, a pupil has shown himself able to do considerably more work than his classmates, he is taken from his class and placed with the one next in advance. On the contrary, if a pupil, through incompetence or indolence, falls behind his classmates, he is taken down to the next lower class.

On the supposition that this entire school is in charge of one teacher, what amount of work will he have on hand? Each subdivision is separated from the next by one year's work. Consequently, each of the twelve subdivisions will furnish four distinct sets of classes, making, in all, forty-eight recitations a day. On the average, this will allow about eight minutes to every class. Of course such a scheme is impracticable. If one teacher should take two of these grades in charge, he would still have thirty-two classes, and could give to each but about ten minutes. This is evidently impracticable. These calculations are based on the supposition that a pupil has but four studies, and has but one recitation per day in each; and that six hours a day are devoted exclusively to recitation. Let us now imagine each of these grades as occupying a room by itself, in charge of one teacher. What attention can be devoted to each recitation?

The most favorable circumstances will furnish the following data: (1) Five and a half hours a day devoted to class-work. (2) In the primary grade, each pupil will have five recitations; in the grammar grade, four; and in the high school, three. The following table will exhibit the essential facts in each case:

Grade.	No. of Recitations to each Pupil.	Whole No. of Classes.	Length of Recitations.
Primary.	5	20	16 m.
Grammar.	4	16	20 m.
High School.	3	12	27 m.

45. Data to be used in grading.—The above calculation will serve to illustrate some of the limitations which are to be taken into account in practical grading. Some of the data which must be employed in arranging a scheme of graded instruction are, for all practical purposes, fixed quantities; others are variable, and, in calculating results, values must be assigned them. Thus it is evident that in cases where but one teacher can be employed the time which he can devote to class instruction is a fixed quantity, not absolutely the same in all cases, but determinable in each special case by taking from the entire session the time needed for opening exercises, roll-call, and recesses. So also the average time which shall be given to each recitation ought to be fixed within very narrow limits. Thus, in primary schools, 15 minutes, on the average, should be the minimum; in grammar schools it should not be less than 25 minutes; and in high schools not less than 40 minutes. To make a convenient use of these data, let us employ the following notation:

T = The whole time devoted to recitations by one teacher.
t = The average length of each recitation.
N = The whole number of recitations.
n = The average number of recitations to each pupil.
Y = The years in the course.

These quantities will give rise to the following equation:

$$(1) \quad T = N \times t = (n \times Y)\, t.$$

As just stated, T and t are virtually fixed quantities, so that n may be made determinate by assigning a value to Y; and Y determinate by assigning a value to n. That is, if we assume that there must be a certain number of years in the course, the average number of recitations which each pupil may have is limited; and, if we start with the last fact, we are compelled to fix on a definite number of years which the course shall occupy. To illustrate the application of these principles to the grading of primary schools, let us make use of two derived equations as follows:

$$(2) \quad n = \frac{T}{Y \times t}. \qquad (3) \quad Y = \frac{T}{n \times t}.$$

Here $T = 5\frac{1}{2}$; $t = \frac{1}{4}$. Now, if we are determined to have four years in the course, the average number of recitations which each pupil may have will be found from the second equation as follows:

$$n = \frac{5\frac{1}{2}}{4 \times \frac{1}{4}} = 5\frac{1}{2}.$$

If, on the other hand, we assume that each pupil may have six recitations, the number of years in the course will be determined from the third equation as follows:

$$Y = \frac{5\frac{1}{2}}{6 \times \frac{1}{4}} = 3\frac{2}{3}.$$

As the results in such calculations must necessarily be whole numbers, some slight modification must be made in the value of t. If we assign to Y, in the last example, the value of 4, the value of t will be deduced as follows:

$$t = \frac{5\frac{1}{2} \text{ hrs.}}{6 \times 4} = 14 \text{ minutes nearly.}$$

46. Limitations of data.—The calculations which have thus far been made relate to the classification of a single school, in charge of one teacher, with a view to determine, either how many years there shall be in the course, or how many recitations each pupil may have. The limitations are the number of teachers, the time which can be devoted to recitation, and the average length of each recitation. Given these limitations, the purpose has been to show the results which necessarily follow from them. It is necessary to keep in mind the important fact that, in grading schools, we must be governed by the resources at our command. Many things are desirable which are not practicable, and we must often be content to make a garment from a scant pattern.

It will be observed that the limitations which have been placed upon our calculations can ultimately be resolved into the lack of teachers. For, with two teachers, the time devoted to recitations is doubled, and consequently we may either increase the number of years in the course, or the number of studies allowed to each pupil. And again, this limited teaching force is due either to a small number of pupils, or to a lack of resources. In a small school of twenty-five pupils there may be in reality eight grades, requiring at least two teachers, if a strict classification is made; but it is quite sure that all the work must be done by one teacher. In such a case the practical question is, how can the teacher's time be employed to the greatest advantage?

47. Can country schools be graded?—With a fair understanding of the principles which have been illustrated, we are now prepared to discuss a question which has received considerable attention,—can country schools be graded? The school to which reference is made consists of from twenty to forty pupils, varying in age from six to fourteen years, taught by one teacher.

Let us assume the following data:

$$T = 6. \quad t = \tfrac{1}{4}. \quad n = 5.$$

Now $$(3)\ Y = \frac{T}{n \times t} = \frac{6}{5 \times \frac{1}{4}} = 4\tfrac{4}{5}.$$

This will give a course of instruction covering five years, adapted to pupils from six to eleven years of age. This course will take a pupil through the Fourth Reader, and half-way through the Intermediate Geography and Arithmetic. Probably there are many country schools composed of younger children, where such a range of studies will suffice. If so, the school can be graded; but whether the grading can be sustained, will depend on the character of the attendance and on the skill possessed by the successive teachers. The two things which make it very difficult, if not impossible, to sustain a graded course of instruction in such schools are great irregularity of attendance, and the frequent change of teachers, whereby it is almost impossible to follow any settled line of policy. The fact that many pupils attend school but a part of the year, during the winter, perhaps, will make it almost impossible to avoid forming classes not provided for in the graded course; while a frequent change in teachers will, in many cases, defeat the wisest plans. There would be much more hope of introducing a classification into country schools, if teachers in general understood the principles which must be observed in the formation and preservation of a graded course of study. A fair degree of professional skill generally disseminated among teachers, and the desire, on the part of Boards of Trustees, to employ the best obtainable talent, can alone carry into effect that settled line of policy which is absolutely required in order to sustain a systematic course of instruction.

Suppose the grading of a larger school, composed of older pupils, is in question, and that the following data are assumed:

$$T = 6. \quad t = \tfrac{1}{4}. \quad Y = 8.$$

$$n = \frac{T}{t \times Y} = \frac{6}{\frac{1}{4} \times 8} = 3.$$

In this case, each pupil will be limited to three recitations each day; and the course will extend from the sixth to the fourteenth year of his age. It is not to be doubted that an orderly arrangement of studies which permits but this number of recitations is much preferable to that confusion which reigns in most schools of this description. While in this, and in similar cases, a system of grading is theoretically possible, there will be found, as in the first case, disturbing causes which may defeat the plan. I have no doubt that country schools may be graded to the immense advantage of their pupils; but whether the graded system can be sustained, will depend very largely on the skill of those who have them in charge.

48. The grading of a small school.—The art of grading will now be discussed in its application to small village schools, which may be supposed to contain at least the germ of a rational classification. It is obvious that most of the difficulties which are encountered in country schools will meet us in village schools in charge of a single teacher, so that such cases do not require further attention. Let us, therefore, consider the case of a village school of eighty pupils, in charge of two teachers. We will assume that the course of instruction is to cover a period of eight years, extending from the sixth to the fourteenth year. We have, then, provision for a primary grade and a grammar grade, of four years each. To assign a distinct grade to each teacher, would be to make an unequal distribution of pupils; but as the recitations must be longer in the grammar grade, this arrangement will probably make a very fair distribution of labor.

Preparatory to arranging a course of instruction, and a programme of exercises, the number of studies which is permissible in each grade must be determined. Let us fix the average time of recitation at fifteen and twenty minutes, respectively. Then, for the primary grade,

$$n = \frac{T}{Y \times t} = \frac{6}{4 \times \frac{1}{4}} = 6;$$

and for the grammar grade,

$$n = \frac{T}{Y \times t} = \frac{6}{4 \times \frac{1}{3}} = 4\tfrac{1}{2}.$$

The correction to be made for the length of recitations in the second case is computed as follows:

$$t = \frac{T}{Y \times n} = \frac{6 \text{ hrs.}}{4 \times 5} = 18 \text{ minutes.}$$

49. **The arrangement of text-book work.** — The next step in order, is to arrange in tabulated form the text-book work which is sufficient for each year of the course. It may be remarked here that there is considerable diversity of practice with reference to the point in the course at which certain studies should be taken up, for example, geography and grammar. At present, the tendency is to postpone these topics to a later period, devoting the earlier part of the course to a thorough training in reading, writing, and calculating. The art of arts is reading; and to the acquisition of this art the primary grade should be almost exclusively devoted. By reading is meant the art of interpreting written language, and not the art of giving vocalized expression to

thought—elocution. The second art has a value, but is not comparable with the first in point of direct utility. Next in importance to reading are calculation and writing. These three arts should monopolize the time and effort of teacher and pupil during the first four years of school life.

The early introduction of geography and grammar may have been due to the number of books in a series. It may have been thought that the three grammars and the three or four geographies were made to be used; and if so, there was need to begin their study at an early period of life. Now, however, the tendency is to diminish the number of books in a series, and at the same time to reduce the quantity of matter which they contain. Simplification is the aim of text-book authors, and the schools are beginning to simplify their courses of study. By reason of the mass of matter which pupils have been forced to learn, the memory has been taxed at the expense of the reason; and in the end, the memory has suffered, for the memorizing of facts merely to be repeated is a dissipation which speedily weakens the power of memory.

There is a striking analogy between the assimilation of food and the assimilation of knowledge. Without noting the most instructive of these analogies, it is sufficient, in this place, to remark that both processes require a state of repose in order that the elements which have been appropriated may be incorporated—those into organs and tissues, these into the complex products of reflection.

The amount of text-book work which can be accomplished in each year of the course has been determined, within certain limits, by experience. It is manifestly impossible to tell in advance the amount of matter which is required; but with experience come needed readjustments of the course; and, finally, these corrections have led to a very general uniformity. There is presented on page 96 a synopsis of a course of instruction suitable for such a school as we have had under consideration. Each column will indicate the work designed for the corresponding year. The figure placed opposite each text-book indicates the point at which a corresponding study begins and ends. Thus the Primary Geography is to be taken up at the beginning of the third year, primary grade, and completed during the fourth year. This synopsis may be changed into a working plan by dividing each column into three parts, corresponding to the number of school terms, and placing figures to denote the page of each book which must be reached at the end of each term. This form will be given further on [page 105].

It is to be remarked, with reference to this synopsis, that in the supposed case only an imperfect grading is possible. In fact, this is but one remove from an unclassified school; and, speaking physiologically, the type of organization is low, because the degree of differentiation is slight. It is no more possible to introduce a high organization into such a school than into a manufactory of guns where only two workmen are employed.

In a highly classified school, eight teachers would be differently employed in doing the work which must be done by two in the case supposed. Is it worth while to grade a school under such circumstances? This is to ask whether an imperfect classification is better than none. Even in case there is no probability that the school will grow, it is well to have at least a rude organization which shall give to it some consistency and shape; while, if there is steady growth in numbers, this imperfect organization is easily developed into others which are successively higher. This statement will be illustrated further on.

SYNOPSIS OF A COURSE OF STUDY FOR AN IMPERFECTLY GRADED SCHOOL OF EIGHTY PUPILS IN CHARGE OF TWO TEACHERS.

TEXT-BOOK.	PRIMARY GRADE.				GRAMMAR GRADE.			
	D 1st Year.	C 2d Year.	B 3d Year.	A 4th Year.	D 5th Year.	C 6th Year.	B 7th Year.	A 8th Year.
Harvey's Graded-School First Reader.	{ }							
Harvey's Graded-School Second Reader.		{	}					
Harvey's Graded-School Third Reader.			{	}				
Harvey's Graded-School Fourth Reader.					{	}		
Harvey's Graded-School Fifth Reader.							{	}
Harvey's Graded-School Primary Speller.		{	}					
DeWolf's Speller.				{				}
Eclectic Primary Geography.			{	}				
Eclectic Intermediate Geography.					{		}	
White's Primary Arithmetic.		{	}					
White's Intermediate Arithmetic.				{		}		
White's Complete Arithmetic.							{	}
Harvey's Practical Grammar.						{		}
Venable's United States History.								{ }
Eclectic Copy Books.			Primary.	1. 2.	3. 4.	5. 6.	7. 8.	7. 8.

50. The arrangement of programmes.—The third and last step is to prepare a programme of exercises for each grade. At best, the teachers of such a school will be over-crowded with work; but on this account there is the more need that their work should be systematic. Time which is to be spent in so many duties must be rigorously subdivided; otherwise, one task will encroach on another, and entail a general confusion. The data for arranging the programmes (pp. 98, 99) are the calculations previously given (§ 48), and the synopsis of studies. It will be observed that by combining two classes in writing and spelling, there is room on each programme for opening exercises and roll call, while there are twenty-two recitations in the first case and twenty in the second. Other modifications of this general plan may be made at discretion. In practice, the spaces not filled may be made to include topics which are to be studied in a fixed order. These have been omitted in order to avoid any danger of confusion.

51. The development of a provisional classification.—Whenever the growth of a school requires the employment of an additional teacher, the original organization should be so modified as to allow a sharper classification of pupils. This should be the guiding principle in making the successive modifications of the system which are required by gradual additions to the enrollment.

School statistics, from whatever source, exhibit one universal law,—that attendance steadily diminishes as we pass from the lower grades to the higher. This general law affords us only a qualitative prevision. With reference to any given school, we can predict with certainty that the high school enrollment is only a small percentage of the aggregate enrollment; though, given the aggregate enrollment, we are unable to state, except within wide limits, the number of pupils who

PROGRAMME OF RECITATIONS FOR THE PRIMARY GRADE OF AN IMPERFECTLY GRADED SCHOOL.

9 to 9-10.	OPENING EXERCISES.			
	D CLASS. FIRST YEAR.	C CLASS. SECOND YEAR.	B CLASS. THIRD YEAR.	A CLASS. FOURTH YEAR.
9-10 to 9-25.	Reading.			
9-25 to 9-40.		Reading.		
9-40 to 9-55.			Reading.	
9-55 to 10-10.				Reading.
10-10 to 10-25.	Oral Instruction.			
10-25 to 10-40.		Arithmetic.	Recess.	Recess.
10-40 to 10-55.	Recess.	Recess.	Writing.	Writing.
10-55 to 11-10.	Reading.			
11-10 to 11-25.	(Dismissed.)	Reading.		
11-25 to 11-40.		(Dismissed.)	Arithmetic.	
11-40 to 11-55.				Arithmetic.
11-55 to 12.		Roll Call.	Roll Call.	
12 to 1.		Intermission.	Intermission.	
1 to 1-15.	Reading.			
1-15 to 1-30.		Reading.		
1-30 to 1-45.			Reading.	
1-45 to 2.				Reading.
2 to 2-15.	Oral Instruction.			
2-15 to 2-30.		Arithmetic.	Recess.	Recess.
2-30 to 2-45.	Recess.	Recess.	Geography.	
2-45 to 3.				Geography.
3 to 3-15.	Reading.			
3-15 to 3-30.	(Dismissed.)	Reading.		
3-30 to 3-45.		(Dismissed.)	Spelling.	Spelling.
3-45 to 4.	Roll Call.	Roll Call.	Roll Call.	Roll Call.

PROGRAMME OF RECITATIONS FOR THE GRAMMAR GRADE OF AN IMPERFECTLY GRADED SCHOOL.

9 to 9-10.	OPENING EXERCISES.			
	D CLASS. FIRST YEAR.	C CLASS. SECOND YEAR.	B CLASS. THIRD YEAR.	A CLASS. FOURTH YEAR.
9-10 to 9-28.	Reading.			
9-28 to 9-46.		Reading.		
9-46 to 10-4.			Arithmetic.	
10-4 to 10-22.	Recess.	Recess.		Arithmetic.
10-22 to 10-40.	Arithmetic.			
10-40 to 10-58.		Arithmetic.	Recess.	Recess.
10-58 to 11-10.			Writing.	Writing.
11-10 to 11-25.	Writing.	Writing.		
11-25 to 11-43.			Geography	
11-43 to 12.				History.
12 to 1.	Intermission.	Intermission.	Intermission.	Intermission.
1 to 1-18.	Reading.			
1-18 to 1-36.		Grammar.		
1-36 to 1-54.			Grammar.	
1-54 to 2-12.				Grammar.
2-12 to 2-30.	Geography.			
2-30 to 2-48.		Geography.	Recess.	Recess.
2-48 to 3 6.	Recess.	Recess.	Reading.	
3-6 to 3-24.				Reading.
3-24 to 3-42.	Spelling.	Spelling.		
3-42 to 4.			Spelling.	Spelling.
4 to 4-5.	Roll Call.	Roll Call.	Roll Call.	Roll Call.

are enrolled in the high school. When this law has been established for a particular school, however, it is in most cases subject to but slight variations, and may lead us to quantitative results within quite narrow limits.

This general law of attendance has an important bearing on the subject now under consideration. While we are certain that increments in attendance will chiefly affect the lower classes, we are not able to predict what special part of the school will require an additional teacher, as successive additions are made to the enrollment; but as the present purpose is chiefly to illustrate the general manner in which a provisional grading is to be modified to meet the requirements of growth, it will be sufficient to follow the general law which governs school attendance.

Let us, then, suppose that our village school has gradually increased in numbers till each teacher has sixty pupils, and it has become necessary to employ additional help. As this increase in numbers will chiefly affect the primary grade, the division which is now required may be made as follows: Let the D and C classes of the primary grade constitute one school; the B and A classes of the same grade, and the D class of the grammar grade, the second school; and the C, B, and A classes of the grammar grade, the third school. No change need necessarily be made in the course of instruction previously given; but new programmes of recitations will, of course, be required.

Let us suppose that for the first school it is thought best to allow fifteen minutes for recitation to the lower class, and twenty minutes to the higher; and that the whole time devoted to actual class work is five hours. Then,

$$n = \frac{5}{2 \times \frac{35}{120}} = 8\tfrac{4}{7}.$$

Let us make a correction for T as follows:

$$T = n \times t \times Y = 8 \times \tfrac{35}{2} \times 2 = 280 \text{ minutes,}$$

or four hours and forty minutes.

PROGRAMME OF RECITATIONS FOR A PRIMARY SCHOOL COMPOSED OF TWO GRADES OF PUPILS.

TIME.	B CLASS.	A CLASS.
9 to 9-10.	Opening Exercises.	Opening Exercises.
9-10 to 9-25.	Reading (1st Division).	
9-25 to 9-45.		Reading (1st Division).
9-45 to 10.	Oral Instruction (2d Division).	
10 to 10-20.		Arithmetic (2d Division).
10-20 to 10-35	Oral Instruction (1st Division).	
10-35 to 10-45.	Recess.	Recess.
10-45 to 11-5.		Arithmetic (1st Division).
11-5 to 11-20.	Reading (2d Division).	
11-20 to 11-40.		Reading (2d Division).
11-40 to 11-45.	Roll Call.	Roll Call.
11-45 to 1.	Intermission.	Intermission.
1 to 1-15.		Arithmetic (1st Division).
1-15 to 1-35.	Reading (1st Division).	
1-35 to 1-55.		Reading (1st Division).
1-55 to 2-10.	Oral Instruction (2d Division).	
2-10 to 2-30.		Arithmetic (2d Division).
2-30 to 2-45.	Oral Instruction (1st Division).	
2-45 to 3.	Recess.	Recess.
3 to 3-20.	Reading (2d Division).	
3-20 to 3-35.		Reading (2d Division).
3-35 to 3-40.	Roll Call.	Roll Call.

Either of two plans may be followed in arranging such a programme. An entire class may be called up for recitation eight times each day, or it may be divided into two sections, each of which may recite four times a day. It is plain that an individual pupil may receive the same amount of attention in each case; though the second arrangement is preferable when the number of pupils in a class is large. The first plan will give rise to the form on page 101.

The place of all others to learn the art of grading is such a school as we have taken for illustration; and peculiarly fortunate is the teacher who is permitted to conduct a school through the various stages of its onward progress.

52. The successive transformations through which a graded-school may pass.—The following table is designed to present a theoretical view of the successive transformations through which a growing school must pass, from its first rude organization to the complete development of all the grades of the common school course. It is not pretended that, in actual practice, growth will take place at the rate or in the manner here indicated. Sometimes an earlier division of the lower classes may be necessary; and such may be the rapidity of growth, that two or more new schools must be opened at the same time.

SUCCESSIVE TRANSFORMATIONS.

		PRIMARY GRADE.	GRAMMAR GRADE.
80 pupils in charge of two teachers.	First School.	D. C. B. A.	
	Second School.		D. C. B. A.
120 pupils in charge of three teachers.	First School.	D. C.	
	Second School.	B. A.	D.
	Third School.		C. B. A.
200 pupils in charge of four teachers.	First School.	D. ½ C.	
	Second School.	½ C. B.	
	Third School.	A.	D.
	Fourth School.		C. B. A.

250 pupils in charge of five teachers.	First School.	D.	
	Second School.	C.	
	Third School.	B.	
	Fourth School.	A.	D.
	Fifth School.		C. B. A.
300 pupils in charge of six teachers.	First School.	D.	
	Second School.	C.	
	Third School.	B.	
	Fourth School.	A.	
	Fifth School.		D. C.
	Sixth School.		B. A.
350 pupils in charge of seven teachers.	First School.	½ D.	
	Second School.	½ D.	
	Third School.	C.	
	Fourth School.	B.	
	Fifth School.	A.	
	Sixth School.		D. C.
	Seventh School.		B. A.
400 pupils in charge of eight teachers.	First School.	½ D.	
	Second School.	½ D.	
	Third School.	C.	
	Fourth School.	B.	
	Fifth School.	A.	
	Sixth School.		D.
	Seventh School.		C.
	Eighth School.		B. A.
450 pupils in charge of nine teachers.	First School.	½ D.	
	Second School.	½ D.	
	Third School.	½ C.	
	Fourth School.	½ C.	
	Fifth School.	B.	
	Sixth School.	A.	
	Seventh School.		D.
	Eighth School.		C.
	Ninth School.		B. A.
500 pupils in charge of ten teachers.	First School.	½ D.	
	Second School.	½ D.	
	Third School.	½ C.	
	Fourth School.	½ C.	
	Fifth School.	B.	
	Sixth School.	A.	
	Seventh School.		D.
	Eighth School.		C.
	Ninth School.		B.
	Tenth School.		A.

During the successive periods of its growth, the classification of a school should become more and more exact. Limited accommodations and a lack of teachers may at first prevent a strict grading of pupils; but, in proportion as these obstacles are removed, smaller differences in individual attainment should be provided for.

When a school has reached the final stage indicated in the above table, nothing needs to be done, in case of further growth, except to establish parallel schools of the same grade. The common school course of instruction has now received its full development; and, in process of time, the establishment of the high school grade will become necessary.

In what has preceded I have attempted to show the manner of employing the data which must be used in grading an unorganized school. The general impression intended to be conveyed is that, in this art, considerable exactness is both desirable and possible. It has not been thought necessary to enter into a minute explanation of the equations which have been employed. A slight examination will show that the primary equation expresses the exact relation between the several data which must enter into a rational distribution of work. The derivation of the secondary equations is obvious; and the substitution of values for n, t, Y, and T in each case will be readily comprehended.

As the art of grading schools is one of the most difficult, and, perhaps, one of the least understood of a teacher's professional duties, it might very properly form a topic of instruction in the higher classes in normal schools. By employing the simple formulæ given in this chapter, pupils may be shown how to arrange a course of instruction and programmes of recitations suitable for given conditions.

53. Synopsis of a common school course of instruction.—The following synopsis of a course of instruction for the primary and grammar grades of a completely graded school will conclude this chapter.

SYNOPSIS OF A COURSE OF STUDY FOR THE PRIMARY AND GRAMMAR GRADES OF A COMPLETELY GRADED SCHOOL.

STUDIES AND TEXT-BOOKS.	PRIMARY GRADE.												GRAMMAR GRADE.											
	D			C			B			A			D			C			B			A		
	1st Year.			2d Year.			3d Year.			4th Year.			5th Year.			6th Year.			7th Year.			8th Year.		
	Terms.			Terms.			Terms.			Terms.			Terms.			Terms.			Terms.			Terms.		
	1.	2.	3.	1.	2.	3.	1.	2.	3.	1.	2.	3.	1.	2.	3.	1.	2.	3.	1.	2.	3.	1.	2.	3.
Harvey's Graded-School First Reader.	26	49	72																					
Harvey's Graded-School Second Reader.				42	69	107	144																	
Harvey's Graded-School Third Reader.								40	82	123	165	208												
Harvey's Graded-School Fourth Reader.													42	81	118	157	191	240						
Harvey's Graded-School Fifth Reader.																			63	125	179	233	277	336
Harvey's Graded-School Primary Speller.				20	32	42	54	66	80															
DeWolf's Speller.										20	36	56	84	104	124	140	154	R						
White's Primary Arithmetic.				29	62	93	116	144	R															
White's Intermediate Arithmetic.										39	69	87	124	148	171	191	207	R						
White's Complete Arithmetic.																			42	88	134	191	245	312
Eclectic Primary Geography.							14	33	53	65	83	R												
Eclectic Intermediate Geography.													19	35	55	71	88	R						
Harvey's Elementary Grammar.													30	66	89	118	160	R						
Harvey's Practical Grammar.																			36	65	123	170	224	264
Venable's United States History.																			36	78	132	186	248	R
Eclectic Copy Books.							Primary.			1.	1.	2.	2.	3.	3.	4.	4.	5.	5.	6.	6.	7.	7.	8.

CHAPTER VI.

THE ART OF GRADING SCHOOLS (CONCLUDED).

SUMMARY.

The high school grade. Opposition to high schools. The Kalamazoo high school case. The special value of high schools. When the high school grade should be established. Courses of study for high schools. Relation of high schools to colleges. Course of study for a first-class high school. The use of text-books. The interval between classes. The multiplication of classes. The reconstruction of schools. The use and abuse of system. Future high school policy.

THE ART OF GRADING SCHOOLS (CONCLUDED).

54. The High School grade. — In many places of smaller size, the high school grade should not be established; the course should stop with what is known as the grammar grade. As the high school is the most expensive part of the system, it ought not to be organized till there are pupils enough to furnish employment for at least one teacher. Up to this period, pupils who have completed the studies of the grammar grade, and wish to go still farther, should go away to some school where they can have the advantages which can not be afforded at home. It is not true that a community is justifiable in establishing a school of high grade for one per cent of its school population. The same economic principles should be practiced in the financial management of a school as in that of private business. Not what is desirable in itself, but what can be afforded, should be the principle of action.

What has just been said should not be construed as in any way hostile to the establishment of a high school when there is sufficient material to support one. A well developed system of public instruction is no more complete without the addition of a high school than an otherwise well developed man, without the larger brain; and so long as education is regarded as the corner-stone of a representative government, public instruction must do more than teach children to read, write, spell, and cypher. These arts, though indispensable, do not include all that is essential for citizenship. The primary school marks the minimum of instruction — that without which no one is fit for citizenship in a free state; but it is a gross perversion of reason to declare that the state should desert the child the moment he has learned the rudiments of an education. A highly developed state requires a highly developed system of public instruction. The mere ability to read and write may fit men to choose their rulers, but it will not fit them to rule. In a government like ours, where the governed of to-day may become the rulers to-morrow, it is not safe to withhold opportunities whereby all may learn what is needful for taking part in the administration of public affairs.

There is no error in reasoning more common, or more fatal, than that of erecting the results of individual experience into a general law. This error is most common among men whom a wider culture would have emancipated from ignorant prejudices. A man whose early educational opportunities were limited to the resources of a country school, but who, by unusual force of character, has risen to positions of influence, will usually ascribe his good fortune to the lack of better facilities for education, and will argue from thence that high schools and colleges are useless. If, as is probable, such a man is a demagogue, he will rail at schools of a higher order, and will see in them manifest proofs of the corruptions of the times, and of the urgent need of returning to primitive simplicity.

55. Opposition to high schools.—Public high schools are opposed by two widely different classes of men — by the ignorant and bigoted, and by the cultivated who are selfishly interested in schemes of private instruction. Wherever denominational colleges are so weak as to come into competition with public schools, there will be found those who deny to the state the right to provide for the higher education of its citizens. There is a legitimate field for denominational enterprise in establishing schools for special denominational needs; but, at this late day, it is not becoming to force all who thirst for knowledge to take the cup from clerical hands or perish from the want of knowledge. The Church certainly has a right to educate, but it has not a proscriptive right to prevent the State from educating.

56. The Kalamazoo high school case.—A recent decision of the Supreme Court of Michigan has put to rest a question which has occasionally arisen as to the legal right to support a high school by public tax. The complainant's theory was,

1st. That a high school exists in *fact*, but not in *law*.

2d. That only schools in which the primary English branches are exclusively taught can be legally supported by tax.

3d. That there is no law authorizing the employment of a superintendent.

An opinion in this case was delivered in court, Feb. 9th, 1874, by Judge Charles Brown, of the Ninth Judicial Circuit of Michigan. The essential points in the decision are the following:

"The special acts of the Legislature, when construed in connection with the general law, authorize the establishment of the school in question, and the employment of a superintendent whose salary may be paid by a tax upon the property of the district."

"The tax levied upon the property of the complainants for school purposes was levied in accordance with the provision of the constitution."

An appeal was subsequently taken to the Supreme Court of Michigan, in which the decision of the lower court was fully sustained.

The following is a partial abstract of the opinion of Judge Cooley in the case:

"*Taxation for higher education.*—The more general question, legally stated, is whether there is authority in this state to make the high schools free by taxation levied on the people at large. The argument is that while there may be no constitutional provision expressly prohibiting such taxation, the general course of the state's legislation, and the popular understanding of the people, require us to regard instruction in the classics and in living modern languages in these schools as not practical, and, therefore, unnecessary for the people at large, but rather as accomplishments for the few, to be sought after in the main by those best able to pay for them, and to be paid for by those who seek them and not by general tax. It is surprising that the legislation and policy of the state should be appealed to against the right of the state to furnish a liberal education to its youth. We supposed it had always been understood in Michigan that education, not merely rudimentary but in an enlarged sense, was regarded as an important practical advantage, to be supplied at will, to rich and poor alike, and not as something pertaining merely to culture and accomplishment, to be brought as such within the reach of those who would pay for it. Territorial and state legislation on this point may be profitably surveyed.

"The constitution as adopted provided for the establishment of free schools in every school district for at least three months in the year, and for the University. By the aid of these we have every reason to believe the people expected a complete collegiate education might be obtained.

The branches of the university had ceased to exist, and it must either have been understood that young men were to be prepared for the University in the common schools, or that they should go abroad for that purpose, or be prepared in private schools. Private schools adapted to the purpose were almost unknown in the state, and very few, then, had money enough to educate their children abroad. The inference is irresistible that the people expected the tendency toward the establishment of high schools in the primary school districts would continue until every locality capable of supporting one was supplied. This inference is strengthened by the fact that many of our union schools date their establishment from 1850, and the two or three years after.

"*State educational policy.*—If these facts do not clearly and conclusively demonstrate a general state policy, beginning in 1817, and continuing until after the adoption of the present constitution, in the direction of free schools in which education, and at their option the elements of classical education, might be brought within the reach of all the children of the state, then nothing can demonstrate it. Subsequent legislation has all concurred with this policy. Neither in our state policy, in our constitution, nor in our laws are the primary school districts restricted in the branches of knowledge which their officers may cause to be taught, or the grade of instruction that may be given, if their voters consent, in regular form, to bear the expense and raise the taxes for the purpose.

"*Superintendency of schools.*—As to the other question, the power to appoint a superintendent was incident to the full control which by law the board had over the schools of the district, and the board and the people of the district have been wisely left by the legislature to follow their own judgment in the premises."

If the complainant's prayer had been granted in this case, the public school system of Michigan would have presented the curious spectacle of a great university at one extreme, the primary school at the other, and a dead blank between. What beautiful consistency to found that university by a constitutional provision, and then, virtually, to deny to pupils the privilege of entering it!

57. The special value of high schools. — Besides their general utility, there are special reasons why high schools should be cherished wherever they can be legitimately established. They are the most democratic of our public institutions. They offer to the poor and to the rich, on equal terms, a culture which will adorn and ennoble any situation in life. By their influence, the communities in which they are situated may be repeatedly reënforced by accessions of cultivated citizens, so that in the course of a few years the whole tone of society may be elevated. There is scarcely a benefit to society which is comparable to this.

Besides, a vigorous high school is needed to give tone and efficiency to the lower grades, to offer that inspiration to effort which is needed to retain pupils in school.

Finally, as has already been shown (§ 24), the teaching force needed in a graded system is most efficiently recruited from the high school. In this way, a system of public instruction becomes self-sustaining.

58. When the high school grade should be established. — On the average, not more than twelve per cent of the entire high school enrollment will complete the course. If the course of study occupy three years, the highest class will constitute one-eighth of the school; the middle class, three-eighths; and the lowest class, one-half. Hence, if, on the average, sixteen pupils enter the high school each year from the grammar grade, the whole enrollment will be thirty-two pupils, forming three classes, of sixteen, twelve, and four pupils, respectively. To conduct such a school properly will require all the time which the principal can spare from his work of supervising, and that of an assistant in addition. It seems to me that a high school should not be organized until there is assurance that at least thirty pupils will be in attendance when the school is in good working order.

I learn from the statistics of forty of the principal high schools of Michigan that, on the average, their membership does not exceed six per cent of the whole school enrollment. Thus our high school of thirty will require an aggregate enrollment of five hundred pupils. I think it may then be assumed that, in general, when the actual school enrollment is less than five hundred, the high school grade ought not to be established.

The statement is subject to some ambiguity from the fact that so called high schools differ so much in their character. I shall assume that a high school, properly called, should have a course of study sufficient to prepare pupils for the scientific course in first-class colleges. A department of this kind will require a course of study for three years, embracing higher English, higher mathematics, and the natural sciences.

59. Courses of study for high schools. — The synopsis on the following page is designed to present a course of instruction suitable for a third-grade high school.

When the aggregate attendance is from eight hundred to one thousand, there may be two courses of instruction, offering to pupils some choice in the selection of their studies. It may be remarked here, that the high school should be popularized by adapting the course of instruction to the varied needs and preferences of its pupils. Every

SYNOPSIS OF A COURSE OF STUDY FOR A THIRD-GRADE HIGH SCHOOL.

	FIRST TERM.	SECOND TERM.	THIRD TERM.
FIRST YEAR.	Book-keeping. Algebra. Arithmetic.	Analysis. Algebra. Physical Geography.	Analysis. Algebra. Physical Geography.
SECOND YEAR.	History. Algebra. Geometry.	History. Natural Philosophy. Geometry.	History. Natural Philosophy. Geometry.
THIRD YEAR.	English Literature. Chemistry. Physiology.	English Literature. Chemistry. Rhetoric.	English Literature. Political Science. Astronomy.

proper inducement should be held out to encourage pupils to persevere in their studies till they can be graduated from the high school. For this reason, it is well to restrict the course to three years in cases where the school is small, and where there has not yet been developed that *esprit de corps* which of itself is an invaluable incentive to perseverance.

On the opposite page is a synopsis of two courses of study for what may be called a second-grade high school.

60. Relation of high schools to colleges.—In states where the public school system culminates in a university, there should be a system of preparatory schools, like the Foundation Schools of England, which will fit pupils for entering on a collegiate course of instruction. A spirit of unity and consistency should so pervade a system of instruction that it may be equally good for the pupil who stops at the end of any given period and for the pupil who continues his studies into or through a higher grade. That is, a grammar school course should be of such a character as to afford the greatest advantage to the pupils who leave

SYNOPSIS OF TWO COURSES OF STUDY SUITABLE FOR A SECOND-GRADE HIGH SCHOOL.

		LATIN COURSE.	ENGLISH COURSE.
FIRST YEAR.	1st Term.	Latin. Algebra. Analysis.	Book-keeping. Algebra. Analysis.
	2d Term.	Latin. Algebra. Physical Geography.	Analysis. Algebra. Physical Geography.
	3d Term.	Latin. Algebra. Physical Geography.	Arithmetic. Algebra. Physical Geography.
SECOND YEAR.	1st Term.	Latin. Algebra. Plane Geometry.	History. Algebra. Plane Geometry.
	2d Term.	Latin. Natural Philosophy. Plane Geometry.	History. Natural Philosophy. Plane Geometry.
	3d Term.	Latin. Natural Philosophy. Solid Geometry or Zoology.	History. Natural Philosophy. Botany.
THIRD YEAR.	1st Term.	Latin. History. French or German.	English Literature. Chemistry. Botany.
	2d Term.	Latin. History. French or German.	English Literature. Chemistry. Physiology or Rhetoric.
	3d Term.	Latin. History. French or German.	English Literature. Geology or Analytical Chemistry. Astronomy.

school at the end of this period, and to those who are to enter the high school. No one questions the truth of this doctrine when applied to the ordinary common school course; but it is a quite commonly received opinion that a high school course which is arranged with reference to the requirements of a university or college is not the best for pupils who are to take no higher course. If this opinion is well founded, it must be that collegiate instruction is not a logical continuation of public school instruction. If this higher instruction is general and not special, if it has reference to the humanities and not to specialties, there can not be this incompatibility. If, on the other hand, it is true that a preparation for college requires a course of secondary instruction which is not suitable for pupils in general, it follows that the college course is not designed for the liberal education of its students. I assume that the higher education afforded by universities and colleges should be a culture in the humanities, and, consequently, that it should be the natural continuation of the instruction given in the high school. Unless a state university really fulfills the conditions of this relation, it is certainly not a legitimate member of the general educational system, and ought to be reconstructed or abandoned.

It is true, I suppose, that while our public school system is of recent origin, and therefore responds quite fully to the exigencies of modern life and thought, the college is rather a mediæval institution, reflecting the opinions, the culture, and the needs of an obsolete state of socicty. It is for this reason, doubtless, that the college is sometimes felt to be outside the general public school system, and out of sympathy with it. There is no reason in the nature of things why this incongruity should continue; and there seems to be no remedy save in a close conformity of collegiate instruction to the general educational spirit which is abroad among the people, and which has made our public school system what it is.

61. Course of study for a first-class high school.—The schedule on the two following pages presents a synopsis of five courses of study, designed for a complete high school of at least one hundred and fifty pupils, and five teachers.

62. The use of text-books.—It will be observed that all the courses of study which have been presented in this chapter have reference to text-book instruction alone. An opinion has been gaining ground for several years that the use of text-books is an evil, to a greater or less extent; and that oral instruction should be the teacher's ideal. Without doubt, the servile use of a text-book, whereby teaching becomes mere lesson-hearing, is a great evil; but it is even a greater evil to discard the use of books. One great end of popular instruction should be to teach the art of using books. A good school-book should be a compendium of facts and principles which the pupil should learn and which the teacher should amplify and explain. If oral instruction supplement text-book instruction, it is legitimate, even indispensable; but if it is to supersede the text-book, it is employed for a wrong purpose. The actual learning of the text is indispensable to real scholarship; but this text should be illustrated till the truths which it embodies are comprehended, and to some extent understood. It is not sufficient to have an idea floating loosely in the mind; it must be defined and fixed by a word. So it is not enough that pupils have thoughts about a given subject; these thoughts should be embodied in concise statements in such a way that they may be within the power of the memory.

"First the idea, then the word" is a dogma of current pedagogy. If this is a protest against mere lesson-learning

SYNOPSIS OF FIVE COURSES OF STUDY

		CLASSICAL COURSE.	SCIENTIFIC COURSE.
FIRST YEAR.	1st Term.	Latin. Algebra. Analysis.	Book-keeping. Algebra. Analysis.
	2d Term.	Latin. Algebra. Physical Geography.	Analysis. Algebra. Physical Geography.
	3d Term.	Latin. Algebra. Physical Geography.	Zoology. Algebra. Physical Geography.
SECOND YEAR.	1st Term.	Latin. Algebra. Geometry.	History. Algebra. Geometry.
	2d Term.	Latin. Natural Philosophy. Geometry.	History. Natural Philosophy. Geometry.
	3d Term.	Latin. Natural Philosophy. Geometry.	History. Natural Philosophy. Geometry.
THIRD YEAR.	1st Term.	Latin. History. Greek.	English Literature. Chemistry. French or German.
	2d Term.	Latin. History. Greek.	English Literature. Chemistry. French or German.
	3d Term.	Latin. History. Greek.	Botany. Geology. French or German.
FOURTH YEAR.	1st Term.	Latin. Review of Algebra. Greek.	Botany. Review of Algebra. French or German.
	2d Term.	Latin. Rhetoric. Greek.	Physiology. Rhetoric. French or German.
	3d Term.	Latin. Arithmetic and Geography. Greek.	Geometric Drawing or Astron. Arithmetic and Geography. French or German.

SUITABLE FOR A FIRST-GRADE HIGH SCHOOL.

LATIN & SCIENTIFIC.	LATIN COURSE.	ENGLISH COURSE.
Latin. Algebra. Analysis.	Latin. Algebra. Analysis.	Book-keeping. Algebra. Analysis.
Latin. Algebra. Physical Geography.	Latin. Algebra. Physical Geography.	Analysis. Algebra. Physical Geography.
Latin. Algebra. Physical Geography.	Latin. Algebra. Physical Geography.	Arithmetic. Algebra. Physical Geography.
Latin. Algebra. Geometry.	Latin. Algebra. Plane Geometry.	History. Algebra. Plane Geometry.
Latin. Natural Philosophy. Geometry.	Latin. Natural Philosophy. Plane Geometry.	History. Natural Philosophy. Plane Geometry.
Latin. Natural Philosophy. Geometry.	Latin. Natural Philosophy. Solid Geom. or Zoology.	History. Natural Philosophy. Botany.
Latin. History. French.	Latin. History. French or German.	English Literature. Chemistry. Botany.
Latin. History. French.	Latin. History. French or German.	English Literature. Chemistry. Physiology or Rhetoric.
Latin. History. French.	Latin. History. French or German.	English Literature. Geology or An. Chemistry. Astronomy.
Latin. Review of Algebra. French.		
Latin. Rhetoric. French.		
Latin. Arithmetic & Geography. French.		

and lesson-hearing, it is legitimate and timely; but if it is put forward as an axiom of educational philosophy, it is false. It is no violation of a true method to teach the word first, then the idea; first the verbal statement of a truth and then the truth which it embodies; or, even, first the abstract and then the concrete. Both processes are legitimate according to circumstances, these circumstances being chiefly the amount of the pupil's experience and his quickness in detecting the special in the general. To say that all instruction must begin with the concrete, is to cut us off wholly from the past, from every thing in the way of knowledge which comes to us by inheritance. For, the accumulated knowledge of the past comes to us in abstract statements, which, for the most part, we must receive in trust as simple beliefs. It is only in a comparatively few cases that these abstract truths can be verified by individual experience.

Some seem to have a strange misconception of the aim and purpose of public school instruction. Of late the schools have been berated because they do not furnish a "practical" education. It appears to be the theory of some that the education which pupils receive in public schools should be equivalent to an apprenticeship in some art or trade. Now, it is not the province of the public schools to turn out engineers, foundry-men, editors, tailors, lawyers, and shoemakers, but rather to form the material of which "practical" men are made. Presently, some one may cry out against woolen-factories because they do not turn out ready-made clothing. The tendency of the American mind is to estimate all things by the prices which they will bring in the market; and so the education which is not directly transmutable into bread is thought of little worth. The schools should teach the arts which relate to the general conduct of life. In this sense, the highest in which the term can be used, common school education should be practical; but not in the narrow sense of teaching handicrafts. The most useful, the most truly practical art which can be acquired, is that of reasoning dispassionately and accurately upon all the questions which come up for solution in daily life; yet it is certain that the studies which best furnish the mind with this ability have but little direct use in those employments whereby the masses of mankind earn their daily bread.

63. **The interval between classes.**—In the courses of study which have been presented, the interval between classes is one year. Under this arrangement, a pupil who is unable to do the work of his grade must be put back for at least one year; and another, who is capable of doing more work than his grade requires, must jump a year's work in order to be reclassified. It has already been observed that skillful management will greatly reduce the occasions for such reclassifications. It is further to be remarked that, in large schools, there is often a difference between grades which are nominally the same. This difference is not enough to defeat the promotion of its members, but will often accommodate pupils who find it necessary to pass from one to the other.

To avoid the seeming, and, in some cases, perhaps, the real disadvantages of this manner of grading, it is thought best by some that the interval between grades should be but six months.

This arrangement certainly facilitates the classification of pupils, and, in this respect, has an advantage over the other system. It is to be recollected, however, that this manner of grading is not practicable in all schools; although it seems to be assumed by some who commend the plan, that it is of universal application.

In general, it is evident that when the successive steps in

a graded course are reduced to one-half their length, their numbers must be doubled in order to extend over the same space. Sixteen grades of six months each are equivalent to eight grades of one year each. To regrade a school like that described in section 49, would double the number of classes in every department; and unless there are pupils enough in each of the new grades to form at least one school, this mode of grading is impracticable. Thus, each teacher in the school of section 53 would have twice the number of classes as before; and unless there are pupils enough to form two schools, this close grading is impracticable. In a grammar department having a two years' course, in which there are pupils enough for two teachers, say one hundred, there may be four grades instead of two. For, in this case, each teacher may have two classes of different grades, instead of two classes of the same grade. On the other hand, if this department is comprised in a single school of fifty pupils, it is evident that one teacher could not attend to the four grades which the new classification would make necessary.

It is evident that, in order to work harmoniously, the same method of grading must be employed in every department of the school. Thus, if promotions take place in the primary school twice a year, they must occur at the same time in the grammar school; for otherwise there will be a gradual accumulation of grades in the latter department. If two new classes enter a department each year, two classes must pass out each year, otherwise the school will be thrown into disorder. It is the usual custom, I think, to graduate classes from the high school but once a year; and in such cases, two classes can not enter it each year without doing violence to the system. Of course this objection will not appear in those schools which are not large enough to support a high school; but in schools of this size, the closer grading is impracticable.

Recent discussions of the graded-school system, and criticisms on its stereotyped methods, have induced some superintendents to reduce the interval between classes to ten weeks. Even where such an arrangement is practicable, it is difficult to see its necessity or utility. Surely there is not such an inequality among pupils as to require these frequent readjustments. If there be pupils whose rate of progress differs so much from that of the multitude, their number must be exceedingly small; and the plan of the school ought not to be adapted to their exclusive needs and thus ignore the good of the greater number. For it is manifestly true, that when classes are reconstructed so frequently, the school will be kept in a state of unstable equilibrium—pupils will not pursue the even tenor of their way, but will be tempted to do superficial work in order to outstrip their classmates. Such frequent reclassifications are not only unnecessary but positively injurious.

64. The multiplication of classes. —Attention may here be called to a fact of importance. There is always danger of multiplying grades in the primary department. Beginning classes must be organized at least twice each year, and if such classes are not merged into one during the year, there will be a gradual increase in grades. The one general plan to follow is to place the older and more capable members of the first class with an advanced class, and the younger and less advanced with the class which last entered the department. Usually, this course can be followed without doing violence to the interests of any pupil. At least, here, as every-where, the good of the greatest number must be respected. The multiplication of grades must be prevented at all hazards; for if it is allowed, it will soon involve the whole school, and lead to the virtual abandonment of the graded system.

65. The reconstruction of schools. — For the sake of simplification, it has been assumed that the reader is interested in the gradual evolution of a completely graded-school out of a small, unorganized school. The object has been chiefly to show the mode of development, the principles which are involved in grading, and finally the model of a thoroughly graded-school. It will not often happen that a man will be called upon to conduct a school through such marked periods of growth. Usually this work is done gradually, by successive hands; but it is all-important, as a necessary preliminary to any variety of successful supervision, to have a well-defined notion of what a graded-school should be. Without such an ideal, it will not be possible, either to reconstruct a degraded-school, to keep up a good classification already made, or to carry forward the classification of a growing school.

Assuming that enough has been said with reference to the gradual building up of a school, it may not be amiss to add some suggestions relative to the reconstruction of a school which, for whatever cause, has lapsed into some degree of disorganization; to holding a school in the even tenor of its way; and to carrying forward a classification already begun. Graded-schools sometimes fall into decay through the lack of good supervision. Unless there is constant vigilance, grades will multiply, first in the primary department, and finally throughout the entire school, till the classification has been destroyed. Teachers will sometimes hold back classes from promotion merely because they dislike to part with favorite pupils, and in this way a disorganizing element is introduced. Again, some superintendents and principals favor a loose classification, which, in the end, means an abandonment of the graded system. But whatever the cause of the trouble may be, it is necessary to know what general line of policy it is best to follow.

(1) If there is not a course of study regularly drawn up, or if there is a course which is manifestly imperfect, one should be arranged and printed, so that pupils, teachers, and parents may know what work will be required.

(2) Ascertain with as much exactness as possible the positions of all the classes in school (Blank § 87), and then rearrange the classes and departments with reference to the course of study. At best, such an organization is merely an approximation to what should ultimately be attained.

(3) During the year watch attentively the progress of the classes, and if it is discovered that pupils are well up with their grade-work in some studies, but are lagging in others, withdraw attention somewhat from the first and give it to the second.

(4) At the close of the year, ascertain the standing of pupils with still greater exactness, and bring the classes into still greater conformity to the course.

(5) Make promotions simultaneously throughout the school, and prevent a multiplication of classes in the primary grades.

When a superintendent or principal comes in charge of a school which is in good condition, no radical change should be made in the general line of policy. If, as is probable, some feature of the system needs to be brought into greater efficiency, develop this part of the school. At any rate, make no haste to introduce changes, unless it is plain that there is pressing need of them. It is a false notion to take for granted that a predecessor's work is full of flaws which must be repaired. It is a great wrong to attempt to establish a reputation by casting discredit on the quality of the work which has been done. Rather than to tear down, the policy should be to strengthen, to develop, the existing system. A needless change in general management is of itself a disaster; but it is made unnecessarily great by overturning the system left by a predecessor. The usual sequence of such a step is a radical alteration in the course of instruction, a change in text-books, and a widely different line of general policy. This is one of the greatest evils from which our schools suffer. It has its origin, to a great extent, in crude notions of the art of school supervision, and it will gradually disappear as school boards, teachers, and superintendents become informed of the general principles which should be followed in work of this nature.

66. The use and abuse of system.— In concluding this portion of my work, I am reminded that something should be said of the abuses which are made of systems in general and of the graded system of schools in particular. In general, systems are useful in proportion as they are administered with intelligence and prudence; and they become mischievous when they are allowed to work by virtue of some inherent power which they are supposed to possess. Even a machine which breaks stone needs intelligent oversight; much more a system which has for its object the training of human beings endowed with intellects and wills. Of all systems, a school will soonest lead to disaster when left to itself. At every moment there is needed the quick eye and the ready hand in order to secure that harmony of movement which is all-essential. There is not an hour in the day in which some event does not occur which, if not properly adjusted, will derange some portion of the system: and a repetition of such cases will ultimately lead to ruin. It is unjust to charge mere system with either praise or blame. It is a machine which grinds well or ill, according as it is managed well or ill.

It is sometimes said that a system is a good thing provided it be not pushed too far—if it be not applied with too great exactness. That is, an unsystematic use of a system will do well enough, but the rigorous employment of a system will tend to evil. Here, as elsewhere, "the letter killeth, the spirit maketh alive." It is not system which kills, but the misuse of system, the divorce of intelligence from the channels through which it operates.

Depend upon it, a loose classification, as in section 63, is an evil compared with a close classification, as in section 49. Yet some superintendents think they are entitled to special credit for tolerating a departure from true system, when the only thing required is an intelligent employment of system.

It is a great error to suppose that system requires us to ignore time, place, and circumstances. It is taken for granted that all who are called to administer the affairs of social, civil, or religious organizations have good sense and ability to make all needed allowances for what is exceptional. All systems must necessarily be framed with reference to the general, the ordinary, and not with reference to the special, the extraordinary; and when exceptional cases arise, it is to be presumed that they are to be provided for.

An adherence to mere system should never endanger the health or bodily comfort of children. It is proper that a time should be fixed for the opening of school-rooms; but if, in inclement weather, a child should reach the school before the stated time for opening, he should be allowed to enter rather than suffer bodily discomfort. Similarly, pupils, when once within the school-room, should be made comfortable, even if it is at the expense of some derangement of technical good order.

Rigor in examination should not insist on the same proficiency in every branch of study. All pupils can not do equally well in each of the studies of the course, and if it appears that a pupil has done all he is capable of doing in a given study, and is not so deficient as to defeat the ends of promotion, he should not be kept back from the advanced studies, though his standing in this one branch is low. The editor of the *National Teacher's Monthly* very justly observes that "proficiency in an average of all studies is, after all, the only just method of classification in school."

It is a systematic use of a system to make it bend to the requirements of exceptional cases; and if there is not enough elasticity in it for such purposes it is unnatural, and should be either abandoned or reconstructed.

There is no doubt that the system of graded-schools has sometimes fallen into disrepute through faults in its administration, one of which, probably, is a servile adherence to form, to order, to the love of unity, pushed to the extreme. It is here that "a little knowledge is a dangerous thing." It is something, to be sure, to make a mill grind, but the grinding will be ofttimes bad, if there be not an ability to regulate the machinery to suit the various uses which are made of it.

67. **Future high school policy.**—Two different modes of thought, two distinct intellectual tendencies, two profoundly-felt needs, are striving for mastery in our American high schools. The love of a generous culture for its own sake, a veneration for antiquity, and an enlightened conservatism would model our high school after the German *gymnasium;* while the love of knowledge for its objective benefits, the spirit of business enterprise so intensely American, and that radicalism which turns its back on the past are attempting to embody their ideas of what an education ought to be in the *real-schule.* In Germany, the struggle

between these two modes of thought has led to the establishment of two varieties of high schools: the *gymnasium*, or classical school, in which the ancient languages hold the principal place; and the *real-schule*, devoted particularly to the natural sciences and the modern languages. In the gymnasia are educated the professional men,—clergymen, physicians, lawyers, men of letters; while the *real-schulen* furnish the country with its semi-professional men,—bankers, surveyors, inspectors of mines, engineers, etc.

The general character of these institutions is clearly defined in the following quotation from *Un voyage scholaire en Allemagne*, REVUE DES DEUX MONDES, 15 *Juin*, 1875:

"The gymnasium and the *real-schule* are two schools of the same rank. The progress of the sciences and the changes which have taken place in society have rendered this division necessary. While the gymnasium attains its end by the study of the languages, and especially by the study of the classical languages of antiquity, and secondarily by the mathematics, the *real-schule* turns rather to the present, that is, toward the vernacular tongue and the foreign languages, to which are added the mathematics and the natural sciences; but, as the present can not be understood without a knowledge of the past, the *real-schule* can not neglect the study of history. . . . . In realizing this programme, it will dissipate the error of those who think that it should furnish those varieties of knowledge which are of immediate use in life. Without doubt, the school ought to have a regard for the exigencies of life, and the establishment of the *real-schulen* is to prove that there is this regard; but it must not be forgotten that the school has to do with children, with young people, for whom we should be content to lay a firm foundation in communicating that knowledge which is general and desirable."

The American high school has been formed on the classical model; but it has every-where had to struggle, and still struggles, with the same spirit, which, in Germany, led to the establishment of the *real-schule*. It can not be doubted that the current of American thought sets strongly toward the extreme practical view of education as opposed to classical culture; and most high schools have been constrained to modify the traditional course of instruction, or at least to offer parallel courses of study which are largely scientific. It is needless to say that no nation that aspires after true greatness can dispense with that variety of culture which is communicated chiefly in the classical school; and there is no great nation in such urgent need of this high intellectual culture as ours. At the same time, there is an absolute need of knowledge adapted to the exigencies of daily life, of that culture which is best communicated in the *real-schule*. Our schools of secondary instruction are attempting to respond to both these needs by offering two courses of study, one classical, the other scientific. Can two schools, so dissimilar in purpose and method as the gymnasium and the *real-schule*, be successfully united under one management? I think it is an observed fact that those of our high schools which are really successful in one of these special departments accomplish scarcely any thing in the other; while the testimony of both Germany and France, after an experience of a century in the first instance, is most emphatic on this point; the two varieties of schools flourish only when they are kept distinct and managed by special faculties.

Our true policy would seem to be, to maintain our classical schools apart, wherever there is a concurrence of circumstances favorable for their growth; and, in all other cases, to imitate the German *real-schule*.

CHAPTER VII.

REPORTS, RECORDS, AND BLANKS.

SUMMARY.

The use and abuse of school statistics. Teacher's Monthly Report. Transfers. Half-day sessions. Number belonging. Per cent of attendance. Attendance rules. Warning notices. Suspensions. Summary of attendance. Absolute enrollment. Average per cent of attendance. Average attendance in months. Fluctuations in attendance. School directory. Ages of pupils. Corporal punishment report. Tabulated statement of cases of punishment. Daily programme. Chart of text-book work. Notification to parents. Teacher's class-book. Marking recitations. Record of monthly and term standing. Principal's record of final standing. The school register. Cost of education per capita. Comparative statistics. Concluding remarks on records and blanks.

REPORTS, RECORDS, AND BLANKS.

68. The use and abuse of school statistics.—The intelligent supervision of schools must be based largely on the facts which are developed by the working of the system. In all rational progress, the point of departure must be the actual condition of the schools as revealed by certain classes of facts; and when carefully devised plans have been placed in operation, the direction and rate of the general movement can be ascertained only by a careful scrutiny of ascertained results. It is quite as absurd to direct the movements of a large school without the aid of accurate statistics as to numbers, attendance, etc., as to assume the general management of an army without detailed statements which exhibit its exact condition. Besides, as certain statistics are required by law, it is not a matter of choice whether records be kept or not.

In actual practice, two extremes are sometimes followed. Some superintendents have a taste for statistical reports, and so require blanks to be filled out for almost every imaginable thing; nor is it material whether the facts are of a nature to be used for any definite purpose. The love of system may be carried so far that the mere gathering of facts is an end in itself.

It is a needless waste of time to tabulate certain orders of facts which are merely curious; they have so little relation to the great results of school organization, and so little influence in shaping lines of policy, that they deserve no permanent record.

On the other hand, some schools have no systematic records; nothing which may serve to guide a new administration in comprehending the general situation. Principals and superintendents owe certain duties to their successors; and a most important one is an intelligible record of what has been accomplished. It has happened in more than one instance that large schools have been left without the least record which could be used to throw light on the actual condition of affairs.

Every school, even the smallest, should have some definite system of reports, records, and blanks. These should be contrived so as to yield accurate and important information. They should not be kept as mere curiosities, or as evidence of great statistical ability, but should be as few and as simple as is consistent with real utility.

69. Teacher's Monthly Report.—The blank here presented, or one of similar scope, should be used in every public school, large or small. Some of the items are imperative; all are of great practical interest. It has been thought best to distinguish the various items embraced in this report with reference to sex. This plan seems desirable on the following accounts:

1. The statistical tables authorized by the Bureau of Education require distinct accounts of the whole number of boys and of girls, and of the average daily attendance of each sex. It is therefore necessary to keep distinct accounts of transfers and of the aggregate attendance in half-days.

2. The recent discussions of "sex in education" make it necessary to record the facts of attendance as they relate to the sexes severally. Dr. Clark, reasoning from undisputed physiological facts, draws the conclusion that girls can not

be subjected to the same educational methods as boys without seriously injuring their health. This is a striking example of that *a priori* reasoning which modern scientists have called into disrepute. No one will dispute the fact which the Doctor assumes as the basis of his argument; but to many it is not at all clear that there is any traceable connection between the cause and the assumed effects. Let it be assumed that "identical" coëducation induces poor health on the part of girls. What will be the inevitable result? Manifestly, under normal circumstances, girls will be more irregular in attendance than boys; and, in consequence, their class work will be of a poorer quality. It is plain that we have need of the actual facts in the case. If school records show that the attendance of girls is more irregular than that of boys, then we may very properly look for the cause of the phenomenon. Possibly we may find it in the fact to which Dr. Clark gives so much emphasis.

Teachers should make the proper entries in this report each half-day, immediately after calling the roll. This will insure accuracy and save the annoyance of hunting up the various items in the school register. At the close of each month, all that is necessary to be done is to copy the entries on a new blank, and calculate the items required in the "Statement."

70. Transfers. — Particular attention should be given to columns A, B, and C. It is readily seen that, in cases where a pupil is transferred from one school to another, there is a duplicate enrollment, and that the absolute enrollment can be ascertained only by subtracting the number of such transfers from the aggregate enrollment. It is of prime importance, therefore, to distinguish between pupils who have not been previously enrolled in any of the schools, and others who enter by transfer. Still further, it is necessary to make a distinction between pupils who are received by transfer. For example, suppose we have the following record of enrollment in the grammar grade consisting of four schools, and wish to ascertain the absolute enrollment: "Whole enrollment, 745; received by transfer, 142." It is evident that these transfers may come from two sources,—either from without the grade, as promotions from below or degradations from above; or from within the grade, as transfers from one grammar school to another. Let us suppose the record made as follows: "Whole enrollment, 745; received by *extra-grade* transfer, 82; by *intra-grade* transfer, 60." From this statement it appears that there have been sixty duplicate enrollments in this grade, and that the absolute enrollment is 745 — 60, or 685. It is often desirable to notice the fluctuations in attendance in a given grade; but it is impossible to arrive at positive results unless transfers are distinguished as above. For lack of better terms, transfers from without the grade are called *extra-grade*, and those from within, *intra-grade*.

Nothing but constant vigilance on the part of teachers will secure accuracy in these items. When a pupil enters, the teacher should ascertain whether he has been previously enrolled during the current school year; and in case he is a transfer, she should ascertain whether he comes from a school belonging to her grade, or from a different grade.

Pupils should not be transferred without taking a notice similar to the one on the opposite page to the school to which they are sent.

71. Half-day sessions.—It is important to observe that when the school has been in session only a half-day, the number entered in column G should be only one-half of that in column H or I, as the case may be. The per cent of attendance is found by dividing the sum of column G (which

FORM OF TRANSFER NOTICE.

NAME, ____________	To Miss ____________
RESIDENCE, ____________	*Please to receive* ____________
FROM ____________ SCHOOL	*who is hereby transferred from* ____________
TO ____________ SCHOOL.	*School,* ____________ *Grade.*
DATE, ____________	*By order of* ____________
	____________, 187

shows the number of days which pupils ought to have been in school) by one-half of the sum of columns H and I (which shows the number of days of actual attendance). In case the number belonging is fifty, and there were forty pupils present during the forenoon, while the school was closed during the afternoon, the per cent of attendance for this day would be only 40 by the rule, whereas it should be 80.

72. **Number belonging.**—It will readily be seen that the number belonging on a given day is to be found by adjusting the whole number enrolled with reference to the entries in columns D, E, and F. Thus, if the enrollment on a given day is 44, and one pupil reënters while three leave, the number belonging is 44 + 1 — 3, or 42. This is an item which deserves attention, as it is one of the data employed in calculating the per cent of attendance.

73. **Per cent of attendance.**—Per cent of attendance is the ratio between the number of pupils belonging and the actual attendance. Thus, if on a given day 40 pupils actually belong to the school, while only 30 are in attendance, the per cent of attendance is 75. This item is significant when it shows what portion of the advantages offered by our public schools is really improved. In practice, however, this is one of the most worthless items furnished by school statistics,—worthless because it is often unreliable, being calculated upon different data, and sometimes purposely exaggerated by tampering with facts. Thus, pupils who are temporarily absent are marked "left." In this way the divisor is diminished and the quotient proportionately increased. Again, so anxious are some teachers to make a gratifying exhibit, that pupils actually absent are marked present. This, of course, makes a fraudulent addition to the dividend. It is not at all probable that strictly honest marking will carry the per cent of attendance above 97. Even

under the most favorable circumstances, the temporary absences caused by sickness and unavoidable necessities will, in all probability, reduce this number to 95 or less. Surely it is time that an item which figures so largely in our school reports should be calculated on reliable data; and I see no good reason why there may not be a general agreement upon the manner of computing this result.

The problem will be simplified by recollecting that we ought to deal only with the real facts of attendance. The first fact is the actual attendance in days. There is no excuse for errors in this item. The correctness of the dividend may thus be assured beyond all doubt. The computation of the divisor is not so simple. Here, however, we shall be assisted by simply recording facts. First, there is a clear distinction between "number enrolled" and "number belonging." After an attendance of one month, a pupil may return to a distant city. Evidently he no longer belongs to the school, though his name must be included in the enrollment. Let us suppose that in a school originally composed of 40 pupils, 10 have thus changed their residence. It can not be claimed that the per cent of attendance in this case should be 75; for this number does not show the ratio between actual attendance and the opportunity for attendance. It is the true number belonging, therefore, as distinguished from the whole enrollment, that should constitute the divisor used in computing the per cent of attendance.

The practical difficulty in the case is now reduced to the task of determining when a pupil's membership really ceases; and this difficulty is limited to the single case in which the teacher is ignorant of the cause of a pupil's absence. Pupils who are temporarily absent through truancy, home duties, illness, etc., should not be marked "left." Their absence should be allowed to diminish the per cent of attendance. But pupils whose membership actually ceases through removal, death, suspension, expulsion, transfer, or from other causes should be marked "left." As all obligation to attend school ceases under such circumstances, these absences should not diminish the per cent of attendance.

An observance of the following rules will secure accurate data for the computation of the per cent of attendance:

1. Pupils temporarily absent from school through truancy, illness, home duties, etc., should be included under "number belonging." These absences should be recorded, and should be allowed to diminish the per cent of attendance.

2. Pupils whose actual membership ceases through removal, death, suspension under the rules of the Board, expulsion, transfer, or through any other cause should be marked "left." Their absence should not be recorded, and should not be allowed to diminish the per cent of attendance.

3. Pupils should be marked "left," under rule second, on the day when membership actually ceases.

4. In case it is impossible to ascertain whether a pupil's absence is temporary or permanent, he should be marked "left" when he has been absent for five consecutive school days.

5. Whenever a teacher discovers that a pupil hitherto marked absent has really withdrawn from school, the record should be corrected so as to correspond with the facts in the case.

74. **Attendance rules.**—Great punctuality is necessary in order to receive the benefits of class instruction. The pupil who receives individual instruction may resume his studies where he left them; but when a member of a class has lost a lesson, he has "dropped a stitch" which can not readily be taken up. A graded-school can not prosper without the enforcement of a stringent attendance rule. At best,

much of the ordinary absence is fictitious; and the common school can scarcely confer a greater blessing than to teach the young habits of punctuality and of strict attention to business. Punctuality of attendance should be a condition of school membership; and every school should adopt some regulations like the following:

Absences.—Any pupil who shall be *absent four half-days in four consecutive weeks*, without excuse satisfactory to the teacher from the parent or guardian, given either in person or by written note, shall forfeit his seat in the school. Pupils thus suspended shall not be restored to the school until the parent or guardian shall satisfy the superintendent that said pupils will be punctual in future, and obtain from him written permission for their return.

Character of excuses.—No mere statement that the parent has kept the pupil at home shall be accepted by the teacher as an excuse for tardiness or absence, and unless it shall appear that sickness or some other urgent reason, rendering attendence impossible or extremely inconvenient, has detained the pupil, the excuse shall not be deemed satisfactory.

75. **Warning notices.**—When a pupil is in danger of supension, under a rule like the foregoing, the teacher should send to the parent a warning notice like that on the following page.

In very many instances this notice will prevent the pupil's suspension, and, in all cases, the parent will be forewarned of a catastrophe which is liable to occur, and he may, if he will, take measures to avert it. In general, every proper care should be taken to keep parents fully informed as to any short-comings on the part of their children which are likely to result in trouble. In this manner, in very many cases, prospective difficulties will be avoided; and parents

FORM OF WARNING NOTICE.

The Public Schools of ______________________

______________________ 187

M ______________________

It becomes my duty, by the rules of the Board of Trustees, to call your attention to the sections of the rules in respect to pupils, printed below, and to notify you that ______________________ *is upon the point of suspension under said section. I sincerely hope it will not be necessary to report* ______________________ *to the Superintendent for suspension, but that with your coöperation we may avoid all future violation of said rule.*

I am, respectfully,

______________________ TEACHER.

EXTRACTS FROM THE RULES OF THE BOARD OF TRUSTEES.

Absences.—Any pupil who shall be ABSENT FOUR HALF-DAYS IN FOUR CONSECUTIVE WEEKS, without excuse satisfactory to the teacher, from the parent or guardian, given either in person or by written note, shall forfeit his seat in the school. Pupils thus suspended shall not be restored to the school until the parent or guardian shall satisfy the Superintendent that said pupils will be punctual in future, and obtain from him written permission for their return.

Character of Excuses. — No mere statement that the parent has kept the pupil at home shall be accepted by the teacher as an excuse for tardiness or absence, and unless it shall appear that sickness or some other urgent reason, rendering attendance impossible or extremely inconvenient, has detained the pupil, the excuse shall not be deemed satisfactory.

Any pupil who is habitually tardy or truant, or guilty of open disobedience, or insubordination, or who indulges in the use of profane or improper language, or who makes use of tobacco in any form during school hours, or whose general conduct is injurious, shall be suspended by the principal teacher of the school to which he belongs.

will have no occasion to complain that they were ignorant of the actual situation of affairs.

Generally, the teacher must decide whether an excuse is legitimate or not. If attendance was impossible or extremely inconvenient, the absence should be excused. In some instances, parents may attempt to save their children from suspension by sending excuses which have no real foundation in fact; but even then the teacher should not go back of the parent's word.

Cases will occur in which dishonest pupils will forge excuses, either for themselves or for others. This should be treated as a capital offense, punishable, if need be, by suspension, or even, if repeated, by expulsion.

For tardiness, an excuse should rarely be granted. In nearly every instance it is avoidable by proper diligence.

76. Suspension.—When a pupil has passed the limits assigned in the attendance rule, the teacher has no longer a discretionary power in the case; but should report the pupil, to whoever has charge of such cases, for suspension. This may be done by the following notice:

No. VI.

The Public Schools of______________________

______________*School.* __________*Grade.*

*To*__________________________

I hereby report to you for suspension,

______________________*aged*__________*years, for the*

*following reasons:*______________________________.

____

___________187 ________________TEACHER.

FORM OF SUSPENSION NOTICE.

The Public Schools of____________________

*Superintendent's Office,*____________________187

*M*____________________

*The following Attendance Rules have been prescribed by the Board of Education. I call your attention particularly to the Absence Rule, and take this method of informing you that*____________________ *has been absent*__________*half-days, without satisfactory excuse, and, in obedience to this Rule, is suspended from school for four weeks, or until I shall have received the fullest assurance that*__________*will be regular in future and cause no more trouble.*

My office hour is from 8 *to* 9 *A. M.*

Very Respectfully,

____________________SUPT.

EXTRACTS FROM THE RULES OF THE BOARD OF EDUCATION.

ABSENCE RULE.

Upon the return of a pupil after any absence, the parent or guardian shall give, IN PERSON OR IN WRITING, an excuse stating the cause. If it shall have been the sickness of the pupil, or necessary attendance upon a sick member of a family, or death in the family of the pupil, in either of such cases the absence shall be excused, and so noted in the register. In every case of the absence of a pupil for more than four half-days in any four consecutive weeks without satisfactory excuse to the Teacher for any other cause than those permitted above, the absentee shall, without exception or favor, be suspended from the school by the Superintendent, and the fact reported to the Board of Education at the next regular meeting.

CHARACTER OF EXCUSES.

NO MERE STATEMENT that the parent has kept the pupil at home shall be accepted by the Teacher as an excuse for absence; and, unless it shall appear that the pupil has been detained by sickness, or some other urgent reason, which would render attendance impossible or extremely inconvenient, or which would cause a serious and imprudent exposure of health, the excuse shall not be deemed satisfactory.

Finally, if there is no evident reason for forbearance, the pupil should be formally suspended by notifying the parent of the fact as on the foregoing page.

The power of restoration is most conveniently and most appropriately left with the principal or superintendent. No one else is in so favorable a position to judge of all the facts and bearings in the case. No arbitrary system should be followed in making restorations. If within an hour, there is assurance given by the parent that all reasonable diligence will be used to secure punctual attendance, the pupil should be allowed to return to his school. It is not punctilio, nor the demands of an arbitrary system which is to be consulted on this and on similar occasions, but the greatest good of the pupil and of the school. Sometimes their interests are in opposition; and, under such circumstances, the good of the greater number must be preferred.

In cases of unusual difficulty, the question of restoration should be submitted to the board for decision.

Notice of restoration should be sent to the teacher in a form as follows:

No. VIII.

Notice of Restoration.

To M ______________________________

The bearer, who was suspended under the Attendance Rule, on the ______ *day of* ____________ 187 ,
is hereby restored to school.

Respectfully,

______________ 187 ______________________ SUPT.

77. Summary of attendance. — For convenience of reference, the "statements" embraced in the monthly reports should be tabulated. The blank form which follows is conveniently arranged for this purpose. These blanks should be of sufficient width to contain the statistics of all the schools of the same grade. Thus, if there are twelve primary schools, eight grammar schools, and a high school, four blanks will be needed to tabulate each month's statistics; and it will be found very convenient in practice to use a fifth blank for a "summary," which shall exhibit the aggregate statistics of each department, and the grand total of all the statistics for the month. This last sheet will exhibit the exact condition of the schools, as to attendance, at the close of each month; and, at the close of the year, will show at a glance the grand summary of all the results.

When the number of schools does not exceed fifteen, perhaps the better plan is to have the blank wide enough to contain, in a single page, the statistics of each month.

It is a good plan, at the end of each year, to arrange these sheets in serial order and have them bound. The successive volumes are invaluable as sources of exact information on material points in the history of the school. From them may be learned the names of teachers; their departments; the attendance in each grade, in each school; the aggregate enrollment; the absolute enrollment; the whole number of boys and girls; the fluctuations in attendance in every part of the system; the average daily attendance; the average time each pupil has attended school; the per cent of attendance of boys, of girls, and of the school as a whole. No superintendent or principal should neglect, even at considerable personal expense, to carry into effect such a simple system as this. It is indispensable for intelligent supervision, and is a priceless treasure to successors in office.

By reason of a separate account which is kept of the items relating to each sex, this blank is somewhat longer than convenience alone would require; but this objection may be removed by folding the blank in the middle. It may then be bound in the same manner as a double page map. Some may not think it worth while to keep up the distinction of items under "Average Number Belonging," and "Average Daily Attendance."

78. **Absolute enrollment.**— In order to obtain the absolute enrollment from the "Summary," subtract the sum of the 13th column from the sum of the 4th column. To find the absolute enrollment in a given grade, subtract from its whole enrollment the "intra-grade" (§ 70) transfers. The general accuracy of the "Summary" may be tested by adding to the "Whole Number Enrolled" the number of "Reëntries," and subtracting from this sum the "Number Left." The remainder should be the "Number Belonging" on day of date. If there is a discrepancy between these results, there is either an error in adding or an error in some teacher's report. In the latter case, test the consolidated report of each department, as above, and when the error has been traced to its general source, turn to the records of this department and test each teacher's report till the exact place of the error is discovered.

79. **Average per cent of attendance.**—The average per cent of attendance should be found not by taking an average of the averages as given in columns 35, 36, and 37, but by dividing one-half of the 26th, 27th, and 28th columns, respectively, by the sum of the 23d, 24th, and 25th columns, respectively.

80. **Average attendance in months.** — To find the average number of months which each pupil has attended school, reduce the aggregate attendance in half-days to

school months (by dividing by forty), and divide this result by the absolute enrollment, which, of course, is the whole enrollment less the "Transfers."

81. Fluctuations in attendance.—Fluctuations in enrollment, number belonging, average number belonging, and average daily attendance, may be graphically exhibited as in the following diagram:

Sept. Oct. Nov. Dec. Jan. Feb. Mar. Apr. May June

1575
1550
1525
1500
1475
1450
1425
1400
1375
1350
1325
1300
1275
1250
1225
1200
1175
1150
1125
1100
1075
1050
1025
1000
975

Enrollment
1211 1256 1288 1307 1375 1395 1401 1542 1571 1574

Average Number Belonging
1143 1134 1130 1114 1104 1097 1106 1114 1116

No. Belonging
1133 1122 1103 1041 1057 1087 1056 1182 1068

Average Daily Attendance
1062 1055 1048 1016 1019 1009 1018 1126 1018

By doubling the number of lines, these fluctuations may be exhibited in their relation to sex.

This is not a mere curiosity, but a striking exhibition of important facts in their relation to one another and to the different portions of the school year. By means of colored pencils, the four items above represented may be vividly exhibited on one page; and a series of such charts would form a most interesting and valuable record.

82. School Directory. — It is very desirable to obtain a complete directory of all the pupils enrolled in a public school. Occasions are ever occurring in which it is necessary to ascertain one or more facts relative to a pupil, such as his residence, the names of his parents, his age, his grade, to what building he belongs, etc., etc.

At the opening of the year, and subsequently as new pupils enter the school, it is an excellent plan to require each pupil to fill out a blank similar to the following:

No. X.

My name is ______________________________,

My father's name is ________________________,

My age is ____________ *years,* ____________ *months,*

I live on ____________ *street, No.* ____________.

As soon as possible after the filling of these blanks, each teacher should embody the items in a form similar to the following (No. XI.), arranging the names in alphabetical order. These lists should then be sent to some designated place for copying into a permanent record.

PUPILS ENROLLED IN THE PUBLIC SCHOOLS OF ....

For the Year 187

.... Teacher.

NAME OF PUPIL.	NAME OF PARENT.	PARENT'S RESIDENCE.	AGE.	BUILDING.	GRADE.	REMARKS.

83. Ages of pupils.—An interesting item of school statistics is the respective ages of the pupils enrolled in the several grades. The following table, No. XII, presents a convenient form for recording facts of this kind.

From such a table there may be learned the whole number of pupils of each specified age; the average age of the pupils in each class of the several grades; the average age of the pupils in each grade, and of the pupils as a whole. The general fact revealed by such statistics is the early withdrawal of pupils from school. It appears from the report of one of the largest school systems in the West, that pupils from six to nine years inclusive constitute 52.8 per cent of the whole enrollment; those from ten to thirteen, 36.2 per cent; and those from fourteen to seventeen, and over, 11 per cent. Different schools will of course give somewhat different results; and it is probably true that the average age of pupils in smaller towns is greater than that of pupils in corresponding grades in the larger cities.

It is important for superintendents to watch the fluctuations in the ages of the pupils enrolled in the several classes and grades. In truth, this is one of the most delicate tests of the working of a school system. If there is a gradual fall in the average age, it may be due to an improved quality of instruction whereby pupils make more rapid progress; or it may arise from the fact that there is not matter enough in a part of the course of instruction. If the average age rises, the fact may be due to opposite causes, or it may result from some change in the circumstances of the community whereby older children are kept in school for a greater length of time. At least it is certain that some causes are at work, which it is well to know.

Great regularity should be observed in compiling statistics relative to the ages of pupils. Not only should the ages be taken in some uniform manner, as in years or months, or with reference to the nearest birthday; but they should all be taken with reference to a fixed period, as the opening of the school year, its close, or some intermediate point, as January 1. If teachers follow different methods, an element of uncertainty will be introduced into these statistics. Perhaps the simplest method is to take each pupil's age at his nearest birthday, reckoning from January 1.

The items for table No. XII may be gathered from the various schools by the use of the form on page 155, which may be filled out at the close of each year from the school register.

84. Corporal punishment report.—When teachers inflict corporal punishment, several good results will come from requiring a written report of each case. All are agreed that this mode of punishment should be reduced to its minimum of frequency; and if teachers know that they must make a statement of each case, showing the offense, the degree of punishment, etc., etc., they will exercise the greatest caution in administering this mode of correction. Merely as a wholesome check on the use of the rod, such a statement should be required.

A still further advantage is the means thus afforded the principal or superintendent of knowing the facts in cases where complaint is made.

No. XIV, on page 156, is suggested as a convenient form for such a statement. It is borrowed from Supt. Rickoff, of Cleveland.

85. Tabulated statement of cases of punishment.—From a collation of such reports, facts of great significance may be elicited. Thus from statements of this character, extending over a series of years, and embracing a large number of cases, I find the following facts as to the

NUMBER OF PUPILS

AT THE RESPECTIVE AGES.

______________________ *Grade,*

______________________ *Class,*

______________________ *Teacher.*

AGES.	BOYS.	GIRLS.	BOTH.	
5 Years, .				
6 "				
7 "				
8 "				
9 "				
10 "				
11 "				
12 "				
13 "				
14 "				
15 "				
16 "				
17 "				
18 "				
19 "				
20 "				

Report of the Punishment of

____________________ (*name*) __________ (*age*)

______________________________ (*residence*)

Date of punishment ____________________ 187

The teacher will please to write answers to the following:

1. *For what offense was the pupil above-named punished?*

____

2. *What is his (or her) general character?*

____

3. *What do you know of the home influences surrounding h ?*

____

4. *What other means have you employed for h reform?*

____

5. *Were h parents duly notified of h conduct before you resorted to corporal punishment?* ________________

What was the nature of the response? ________________

6. *Has ever been referred to the principal of the school or to the superintendent?* ________________

How many times? ________________

7. *What was the result of the punishment?*

____

______________________________ TEACHER.

age at which pupils are most unmanageable. The figures indicate the per cent of the aggregate number of cases which fall under the several ages:

AGES.	6	7	8	9	10	11	12	13	14	15	16
CASES.	1.2	4.8	11	12	18	16.8	15	10.8	7	1.5	1.1

Again, if we group these cases under the departments of the school in which they occurred, we shall have the following result:

	PRIMARY.	SECONDARY.	GRAMMAR.
AGES.	6–9	9–12	12–16
CASES.	29.	50.2	20.8

Finally, if these cases be tabulated under the months and terms of the school year, we shall have the following result:

FALL TERM.				WINTER TERM.			SPRING TERM.		
Sept.	*Oct.*	*Nov.*	*Dec.*	*Jan.*	*Feb.*	*Mar.*	*April*	*May*	*June*
11.	15.6	13.4	8.2	10.	12.6	8.2	9.	7.5	4.5
40.2				20.8			21.		

To say the least, it is evident that these results are not fortuitous. In each case there is a law discernible. With respect to age, it has no doubt been observed by all experienced superintendents that the pupils who are most unmanageable are found in secondary or intermediate schools, but it may not have occurred to all that the troublesome age *par excellence* is ten years. We need not go far to find an explanation for the general fact that pupils from ten to twelve years of age are the most difficult to manage. Mere children have little mastery over themselves, and must therefore be governed to a great extent by authority; but as they approach adult age, there has been such a development of the moral sense and of self-control, that the chief governing force is principle—a regard for what is right and becoming. The intermediate age is a period of transition, in which the child is influenced alternately by authority and by principle; and like all periods of transition from one *régime* to another this is characterized by outbreaks of passion and freaks of impulse, which lead to the necessity of correction.

With respect to misdemeanors which are punishable by suspension, the chief of which is truancy, it is perhaps a singular fact that the culminating period is at the age of twelve.

It will be observed from the last table that the necessity for punishment culminates toward the middle of each term; while, on the whole, there is a steady decline as the year advances. This, doubtless, is owing to the fact that pupils are brought more and more under subjection to authority; and I venture to express the opinion that if such a table were to embody the results of an entire administration by a competent, steady hand, it would exhibit the same law of decline in cases of punishment.

Without doubt, different schools will give somewhat different results; but in every case where a steady line of policy is pursued, the results, such as they are, will indicate some law which it is important to know.

86. Daily programme.—Every teacher should be required to follow a carefully prepared daily programme. This will tend to give system and exactness to school-room work. One copy of this programme should be sent to the principal or superintendent, and another posted in a con-

________________ PUBLIC SCHOOLS.

Central School. **Grammar Grade.**

DAILY PROGRAMME.

FORENOON.

TIME.	LENGTH.	RECITATIONS.
9 o'clock.	5 minutes.	Opening Exercises.
9.5 "	20 "	Writing.
9.25 "	20 "	Reading—1st Division.
9.45 "	30 "	Arithmetic—2d "
10.15 "	30 "	Grammar—1st "
10.45 "	30 "	History—2d "
11.15 "	15 "	Spelling—1st "

AFTERNOON.

TIME.	LENGTH.	RECITATIONS.
1.30 o'clock.	15 minutes.	Reading—2d Division.
1.45 "	30 "	History—1st "
2.15 "	30 "	Grammar—2d "
2.45 "	30 "	Arithmetic—1st "
3.15 "	15 "	Spelling—2d "

________ 187

____________________ *Teacher.*

______________ PUBLIC SCHOOLS.

Central School. Grammar Grade.

POSITION OF CLASSES.

(This Report is to be rendered to the Superintendent at the beginning and middle of each term.)

TEXT-BOOKS.	NO.	CLASS.	PAGE.
Harvey's Fifth Reader.	40	A	190
White's Complete Arithmetic.	"	"	130
Eclectic Intermediate Geography.	"	"	50
Harvey's Practical Grammar.	"	"	118
Venable's United States History.	"	"	125

Dec. 20, 1874.

______________ TEACHER.

spicuous place near the teacher's desk. A convenient form, where a school is composed of a single grade of pupils, is given on page 159.

87. Chart of text-book work.—An important point in school supervision is to ascertain the degree to which each school conforms to the established course of study. This information may be very conveniently collected by means of a blank, called "Position of Classes," which teachers should be required to fill out at stated periods. A report of this kind, furnished by Supt. Doty, is presented on page 160.

The information contained in these reports, if embodied on a single page, will give a complete chart of the text-book work; and is one of the most useful aids to supervision. For its general utility, it should rank next to the "Summary of Attendance;" and whenever the number of schools exceeds ten, such a chart should be constructed. A little skill in ruling will enable the principal to improvise such a blank, if it is not thought best to have them printed in the usual way. A specimen of this chart faces this page.

This chart is of great assistance in making those redistributions of pupils which are necessary at the close of each school year. By this means, a large school may be rearranged somewhat as military forces are distributed by the aid of maps of the seat of war. It is well to have an actual commencement at the close of the school year. The promotions having been decided on, and the material of each school fixed from a careful study of the whole system as revealed by the chart, each pupil should be sent to the place which he is to occupy during the next year. Important advantages are derived from such a practice.

(1). There is the general satisfaction which is felt when a definite arrangement has been made.

(2) The mind of the pupil is in repose, ready for the relaxation which the vacation should bring.

(3) The greater part of that confusion which usually attends the opening of the year is avoided.

A very convenient way to preserve these charts is to have a "stub-book" prepared, of the requisite size, in which these blanks are to be inserted as they are filled out, placing the first one at the end of the book, and the others in succession above it.

88. Notification to parents. — It has already been remarked, incidentally, that it is very desirable to keep parents fully informed of the difficulties into which their children have fallen, or are likely to fall. Education has been too exclusively relegated to teachers; and parents too generally feel that they have nothing to do with the instruction of their children. This I believe to be one of the weak points in the educational policy of the day. Unless the work of the teacher is supplemented by some attention on the part of parents, it is scarcely possible for school instruction to be eminently profitable. The parent should coöperate with the teacher in a positive manner both in the case of instruction and in that of discipline. So far as possible, teachers should become personally acquainted with parents, and thus prepare the way for intelligent coöperation; but as this is frequently impossible, to any considerable extent, teachers should communicate with parents by note or by printed forms. When pupils, through neglect or through inability, are in danger of falling out of their classes, parents should be made acquainted with the plain facts in the case, in the hope that they may stimulate their children to greater exertion, or that, in the event of disaster, they may the more willingly acquiesce in the changes which shall seem necessary.

If parents are not forewarned in such cases, there is just ground to charge teachers with neglect of duty. A blank of the following form affords a convenient means of communicating with home authorities:

XVIII.

_______________ 187

*M*_______________

Your attention is respectfully called to the fact that _______________ *is not doing the kind and amount of work which are necessary in order that he may be promoted with his class at the close of this year.*

The chances of promotion do not depend solely on the final examination, but quite largely on the quality of each day's recitations.

Hoping to receive your coöperation,

I am, very respectfully,

_______________ TEACHER.

It is equally important to warn parents of the bad conduct of their children. In nearly all cases where there is good family government, it is sufficient to notify parents of the misconduct of their children, to have it corrected. It is not meant by this that every trivial matter should be reported in this way; such a course would bring the authority of teachers into contempt. But when pupils show a persistence in bad conduct, which ordinary admonition does not correct, and which promises to result seriously, it is the duty of teachers to notify parents of the facts in the case. Such notifications may be made in the following form:

M ____________________

I am sorry to inform you that
____________________ *causes me considerable trouble by*

____

I have used all the mild means in my power to correct this fault, but thus far with no satisfactory results. Your attention is now called to the matter in the hope that your influence may prevent more serious trouble.

Very respectfully,

____________________ TEACHER.

____________________ 187

In high schools, where the requirements as to class-standing should be more exact (§108), parents should be notified in every instance when pupils fall below the standard. In this, as in all similar cases, it is best to send these notices by third parties, preferably by post, and not by pupils themselves. The temptation to destroy messages which are known to contain unwelcome tidings should be avoided.

89. Teacher's class-book.—In those grades in which promotions are based, in part at least, on the average quality of the pupil's class-work, an accurate record should be kept of each recitation. It is not an easy matter to estimate every recitation at its just value; but when lessons of reasonable length have been assigned, and pupils have been called on to reproduce the knowledge which should have been acquired, a conscientious and judicious teacher ought to be able to assign a value to each recitation with a good degree of accuracy. The mere fact that recitations are marked is a healthy stimulus to industry; and when promotions are known to depend on the average of these marks, pupils feel it necessary to make a steady effort to acquit themselves creditably. There are but few pupils who do not need a stimulus of this kind; and a judicious system of marking will give a tone to ordinary class-work which can be secured in no other way.

It is of considerable importance to decide on a scale of marks. Some prefer 100, some 10, and others 5. The first seems to allow to great a latitude; the teacher is in danger of forming a loose estimate of values. The last is, perhaps, too limited in its range, not elastic enough to represent all the variations in quality which recitations are likely to present.

90. Marking recitations.—The question which should be ever present to the mind of the teacher is: To what extent has this pupil comprehended the truths which are set forth in the lesson which is in process of recitation? The mere fact that a pupil can repeat the very words of the text is in itself no proof that he has comprehended the thought of the author; but when he gives a clear statement of the thought in his own language, there is but little room to doubt the reality of his knowledge. While it is extremely desirable that a recitation should be made in a form which is strictly grammatical, it is not just to lower the marking for mere grammatical errors. A pupil who is reciting a lesson in astronomy should be marked according to his knowledge of this special subject. So, too, in written examinations, only one element should enter into the value which is assigned to a paper on a specified topic. Still less should conduct modify the marks which a teacher assigns to a recitation. Possibly a boy while reciting in grammar may adopt a surly or impudent manner; but if his knowledge of the subject is all that can reasonably be required, his recitation should receive a high mark notwithstanding his bad conduct. This should receive attention in another way.

It is not a good plan to allow pupils access to the class-book. As they are not competent to judge of the grounds on which the marks are based, they should not be allowed an opportunity to call in question their accuracy. For those who adopt a system of examinations similar to the one recommended in section 108, the form of class-book opposite will be convenient.

91. Record of monthly and term standing.—It will be found useful to keep two additional records in connection with the class-book, especially if it is thought best to adopt the system to which reference has just been made. This system turns a pupil's class-work successively into monthly standing, term standing, and final standing. A pupil's monthly standing is derived from the average of his recitations during the month, in connection with the result of his monthly examination. Term standing is derived from the average monthly standing, and the result of the term examination; while final standing is based on an average of the term standing, and the final examination. Each teacher should keep a distinct record of the above items, and should submit it, at stated periods, to the principal of the school, in order that he may take an account of each pupil's final standing. On page 168 is a specimen of a teacher's record of monthly and term standing.

92. Principal's record of final standing.— Finally, there is required in every efficient high school a permanent record of every pupil's final standing. A specimen page of such a register is presented on page 170.

The advantages of such a record are obvious. Its general

Class in

Teacher's Class-Book.

Month of ____________________

(May be extended to include space for from twelve to sixteen weeks.)

NAMES.	FIRST WEEK.					SECOND WEEK.					THIRD WEEK.					FOURTH WEEK.					Average of Recitations.	Monthly Examinations.	Monthly Standing.
	M	T	W	T	F	M	T	W	T	F	M	T	W	T	F	M	T	W	T	F			

TEACHER'S RECORD OF MONTHLY AND TERM STANDING.

CLASS IN VIRGIL.	Monthly Standing. 1874.				Term Examina'n.	Term Standing.	Monthly Standing. 1875.			Term Examina'n.	Term Standing.	Monthly Standing. 1875.			Term Examina'n.	Term Standing.	Final Examina'n.	Final Standing.
	Sept.	Oct.	Nov.	Dec.			Jan.	Feb.	March.			April.	May.	June.				
(*Work done.*)	B.I. 305	B.I. 756	B.II. 402	B.II. 804			B.III. 355	B.III. 718	B.IV. 361			B.IV. 705	B.V 423	B.V 871				
Mary Jones,	8	9	7	9	8	8.1	9	8	8	9	8 6	8	9	9	9	8.8	9	8.7

tendency is to give accuracy and exactness to high school management. It is easy to tell at a glance the quantity and quality of every pupil's work, to tell what studies of the course he has completed, and, consequently, whether he is entitled to the honor of graduation. The full advantages of this whole system will be most fully appreciated when there is a general change in the administration of the school. The three books which have been described have the same relation to the condition of a school as a merchant's day book, journal, and ledger have to the condition of his business; and there is no argument in favor of an exact book account in general business, which is not applicable to the affairs of a high school.

93. **The school register.**—A most important duty of a teacher is to keep a neat, accurate, and legible school register. The facts of attendance should be entered with perfect accuracy, and in such a manner as to be readily comprehended. All the books in a given school should be kept after the same system. The registers should all be of one form, and the entries should be made in the same manner.

It is a saving of time to record the absence of pupils, and not their attendance.

Well arranged school registers are readily procurable from any publisher or bookseller, and no special form need be suggested.

94. **Cost of education per capita.**—It is no discredit to mathematical science to say that figures sometimes lie, not voluntarily, of course, but on compulsion. The ground for thus challenging the truth of a time-honored maxim is the reckless way in which some superintendents manipulate statistics to show at what a cheap rate they supply educational advantages.

PRINCIPAL'S RECORD OF FINAL STANDING.

ENGLISH COURSE.

NAMES OF PUPILS.	FIRST YEAR.					SECOND YEAR.						THIRD YEAR.								
	Book-keeping.	Analysis.	Arithmetic.	Physical Geography.		Algebra.	Plane Geometry.	History.		Natural Philosophy.		Botany.	English Literature.	Chemistry.	Physiology.	Rhetoric.		Geology.	Analytical Chemistry.	Astronomy.

The cost of education *per capita* is one of the least trustworthy items of school statistics. The difficulty lies partly in the fact that there is no settled agreement on the items which should constitute the aggregate cost; and somewhat on a desire to exhibit the comparative cheapness at which education is furnished under particular systems. A large divisor is found in the aggregate number of pupils enrolled; while a small dividend is secured by leaving out of account sundry items of expense, which, nevertheless, must be paid out of the public funds.

It is surely a discredit to our profession that so important an item as the actual cost of educating a pupil in our public schools can not be determined with sufficient accuracy to be used in the comparison of different systems. The National Teachers' Association, seconded by the Bureau of Education, has recently made an attempt to introduce a uniform method of selecting the data for this computation. For the divisor, the average daily attendance is taken. This is surely more just than to take the whole enrollment, since this last number includes many pupils whose actual membership is only a fraction of the school year. If all superintendents would adopt this one item, at least one element of certainty would be introduced into the computation of this important result. As to the items which should constitute the dividend, there is no general agreement; yet it seems that there ought to be no peculiar difficulty in the way of an understanding on this point.

Funds raised by tax for the support of schools are applied in two ways—to defray current expenses, and to make permanent investments. Superintendence, instruction, the care of buildings and grounds, warming, incidentals, repairs, and whatever else disappears in the using, are items of current expense; while under permanent investments are to be included new buildings, libraries, apparatus, and whatever else may serve the needs of successive generations of children. For the sake of distinctness, these items may be tabulated as follows:

School funds may be devoted to	Current expenses.	Superintendence; instruction; care of buildings and grounds; warming; insurance; incidentals, such as ink, paper, crayons, printing, chemicals, brooms, etc., etc., and whatever else disappears in the using.
	Permanent investments.	Buildings; grounds; apparatus; library; permanent improvements; and whatever else may serve the needs of successive generations of children.

It is evident that all items of current expense should be included in the dividend which is to be employed in computing the average cost of education per pupil; but as the benefits of all permanent investments will be distributed among successive generations of pupils, only the interest on the capital invested in school property should be added to the items which are to be included in each year's expense account. I see no reason why the average cost per year of educating a pupil in our public schools should not be computed as follows:

To the items of current expense as explained above, add the interest at the current rate on the true valuation of school property, and divide this sum by the average daily attendance of pupils. This will at least serve as the basis for a comparison of results, and, at the same time, will give, within very narrow limits, the absolute cost of education per pupil.

Let us suppose that by accurate employment of these data it should appear that the average cost of education in one case is $15 per year, and, in another, $18. It is plain that no valuable information can be derived from this bald statement of facts. We want to know what special elements in the computation have given rise to this difference in results. The real significance of statistics of this class can be revealed only by a somewhat minute analysis of the items which constitute the ascertained cost. The following table is designed to suggest the general method by which such an analysis may be made:

ANALYTICAL TABLE.

SHOWING THE AVERAGE COST OF EDUCATION PER PUPIL.

	Average Daily Attendance.	Cost of Superintendence and Instruction.	Cost per Pupil.	Interest on Permanent Investment.	Cost to each Pupil.	Cost of Incidentals, Supplies, etc.	Cost to each Pupil.	Whole Cost per Pupil.
Aggregates	1350	$14,200		$8,000		$4,000		
High School	150	4,000	$26.66		$5.92		$2.96	$35.54
Grammar	500	4,700	9.40		5.92		2.96	18.28
Primary	700	5,500	7.86		5.92		2.96	16.74
Averages			10.52		5.92		2.96	19.40

95. Comparative statistics. — A very important element in modern educational progress is the comparative study of school systems with a view to ascertain the net practical results and the means by which they were produced. This is, in fact, an application of the experimental method which characterizes modern thought; the very opposite of that high *a priori* method which consists in evolving from the depths of the inner consciousness both the general plan and the special methods of an educational system.

To make comparisons possible, uniform data must be furnished—there must be a general agreement on a system of school statistics. At the meeting of the National Teachers' Association, at Detroit, in August, 1874, there was adopted the following schedule of "Inquiries respecting city school systems." The National Bureau of Education has approved this plan, and has recommended it to the attention of all city superintendents of schools. The commissioner of education is rendering invaluable aid in giving shape to our national system of education; and superintendents, for the sake of the common good, should render him the most hearty coöperation.

Inquiries Respecting City School Systems.

1. Name of city, ____________ 2. State, ____________

3. Total population according to census of 1870, ____________

Estimated present population, ____________

4. Legal school age, between ____ and ____ years.

5. Number of school population.
   - Under 6, ________
   - Between 6 and 16, ________
   - Over 16, ________
   - Total number of legal school age, ________

6. Whole number of different children, enrolled in public schools, excluding duplicate enrollments.
   - Under 6, ________
   - Between 6 and 16, ________
   - Over 16, ________
   - Total, ________

7. Number of school days in the year, ________

8. * Number of days the schools were taught, ________

9. Estimated real value of property used for school purposes.
   - Grounds or sites, $________
   - Buildings, ________
   - Furniture, ________
   - Apparatus, ________
   - Total, ________

10. Taxable property.
    - Estimated cash value of $________
    - Assessed valuation of ________

11. Tax for school purposes.
    - Mills per dollar of cash value, $________
    - Mills per dollar of assessed value, ________

---

* This may differ from the "Number of school days in the year" on account of holidays other than those which are provided for in the standing rules of the schools.

	Elementary Schools.							
	Primary schools, for children in the first four years of the school course.	Grammar schools, for children in the second four years of the course.	High schools, or 3d four years of school course.	City normal schools.	Evening schools.	Grand total of city school system.	Private and parochial schools corresponding in scope with public schools.	Grand total of all schools, public and private.
	A	B	C	D	E	F	G	H
12. Number of school-rooms in which pupils are seated for both study and recitation under charge of one teacher.								
13. Number of school-rooms in charge of two or more teachers teaching in the same room or in recitation-rooms.								
14. Number of rooms used for recitation only.								
15. Number of different school buildings, not counting more than one upon a single lot unless they be used for different classes of schools, as for grammar and for high, high and normal, etc.								
16. Number of sittings for study.								
17. Number of teachers, Jan. 1, including principals. — Males,								
Females,								
Total,								

			A	B	C	D	E	F	G	H
18. Average number of teachers employed.		Males,								
		Females,								
		Total,								
19. Number of scholars.	Enrolled.	Males,								
		Females,								
		Total,								
	Average daily attendance.*	Males,								
		Females,								
		Total,								
20. Average daily attendance per teacher, excluding special teachers.										

* To be obtained by dividing the actual attendance by the number of days the school was in actual session, excluding all holidays and days on which all the schools of the city were dismissed.

RECEIPTS.

21. Balance on hand from last school year, $ ______

22. Amount received from interest on permanent funds.
    - State, $ ______
    - County, ______
    - Local, ______

23. Amount received from taxation.
    - State, ______
    - Local, ______

24. Amount received from tuition fees, ______

25. Amount received from all other sources,* ______

Total receipts, ______

* Such as donations, bequests, fines, licenses, sale of property, etc. If any of these go into a permanent fund, the interest only should be reported.

EXPENDITURES.

Item	Particulars	Amount	Total
26. Permanent.	For sites and buildings,	$______	
	For furniture and apparatus,	______	
	For libraries,	______	$______
27. Payment of indebtedness incurred in previous years.	Bonds (including interest),	$______	
	Floating (including interest),	______	______
28. Tuition.	Cost of supervision, including salaries of principals not regularly employed in teaching any class or classes not otherwise provided for, or a due proportion of salary where only part of the time is given to supervision,	$______	
	Amount paid for teaching,	______	______
29. Incidental or contingent expenses.	Officers of the board, secretaries, messengers, etc.,	$______	
	Pay of janitors of build'gs,	______	
	Fuel,	______	
	Rent,	______	
	Insurance,	______	
	Repairs,	______	
	School-books supplied for use of pupils,	______	
	All other supplies and current expenses,	______	______
Total expenditures,			______
30. Average expenses per capita.	Supervision and instruction based on average daily attendance,	$______	
	Incidental or contingent expenses (29) based on average daily attend'ce,	______	

ANNUAL SALARIES.

31. *Annual Salaries of School Officers and Teachers.*

		Maximum.	Minimum.	Average.
Of city superintendent.				
Of assistant superintendents.	Male,			
	Female,			
Of principals in primary schools, no class of which has completed the fourth year's course of study.	Male,			
	Female,			
Of assistants in primary schools.	Male,			
	Female,			
Of principals in grammar schools, the highest class of which has completed the fourth year's course.	Male,			
	Female,			
Of assistants in grammar schools.	Male,			
	Female,			
Of principals in high schools.	Male,			
	Female,			
Of assistants in high schools.	Male,			
	Female,			
Of principals in normal schools.	Male,			
	Female,			
Of assistants in normal schools, including critic teachers.	Male,			
	Female,			
Of teachers in evening schools.	Male,			
	Female,			
Of special teachers.	Music,			
	Drawing,			
	Penmanship,			
	______			
	______			

______187 ______Supt.

96. Concluding remarks on records and blanks.— In what has preceded, attention has been called to such records, reports, and blanks as are deemed necessary for the organization and efficient management of a graded-school. Nothing has been commended to the attention of the reader which is not known to have a real value. It is believed that no first-class school can be successfully conducted without using forms similar to those which have been presented. In fact, I have been governed in this matter by what has seemed to be essential. Very many superintendents will adopt additional forms for special purposes; but as it is not the object of this chapter to present what is merely convenient, or what only peculiar exigencies may require, no mention has been made of forms which are not adapted to general use.

CHAPTER VIII.

EXAMINATIONS.

SUMMARY.

Classification of pupils. The reclassification of pupils. The individuality of pupils. Reclassification may be avoided. A final examination not a fair test. Estimating final standing. Deciding on fitness for promotion. Rigor in examinations. Oral and written examinations. Conducting a written examination. High school examinations. Rules for a system of examinations. Deception in examinations. Herbert Spencer on examinations. The preparation of questions. Examinations to develop general principles. Public examinations.

EXAMINATIONS.

97. Classification of pupils.—It has sometimes been urged as an objection to the graded-school system that it is a sort of a Procrustean bed—that the bright and the dull are submitted to the same process, and that both classes suffer from the regimen to which they are subjected; the first from a cramping of their energies, the second from a strain which their faculties are unable to bear. It is urged that it is a necessary result of class instruction that the individuality of the pupil must be sacrificed to the maintenance of mere system.

Of course all classification is based on some notion of similarity, upon certain points of resemblance; but it is not required that the objects which constitute a class shall be the exact copies of one another. While the classification of pupils is based on certain resemblances, it must necessarily admit certain differences. It is required that all pupils of the same grade shall have attainments so similar that they may derive advantage from simultaneous instruction. It is not necessary that they shall all be on the same absolute level of attainment. If differences of attainment and ability are incompatible with simultaneous school instruction, the objection lies equally against all association for mutual good—social, civil, and religious. A graded system of instruction, wisely administered, is more elastic than any other system of a similar nature; it responds more promptly to the necessities of growth, and admits more easily of those re-adjustments which are required by varying rates of development.

98. Reclassification of pupils.—It is a great error to suppose that a classification made at the opening of a school year must necessarily remain unmodified to its close. As soon as it is discovered that an individual pupil is so much in advance of his class, either in attainment or ability, that he deserves promotion, he is at once transferred to a higher grade; and, conversely, when a pupil fails, through indolence or inability to do the work which is required of his class, he is placed where his deserts entitle him to go. In practice, these re-adjustments are made whenever occasion requires, though these occasions are not so frequent as is imagined by those who are not practically acquainted with graded-school work.

For, first, there are not those marked differences in ability which some imagine, or, at least, the cases of such superiority are far more rare than is popularly supposed. It will be readily seen, even by the inexperienced, that at the end of a school year, there may be such a redistribution of pupils that individual ability may be very exactly accommodated. On the supposition that a normal re-adjustment has thus been made, is it probable that there will be such a sudden evolution of ability as to make a new classification necessary? Or, on the other hand, is it probable that pupils will so belie their past history as to make necessary their transfer to a lower grade? Those critics make a sad mistake who leave it to be inferred that dolts and geniuses are unevenly yoked in the same class.

The differences which actually manifest themselves, and which require special attention, have their origin outside of the graded system; it is very seldom that they are produced within it. The cases of most frequent occurrence in which a higher classification becomes necessary are those of pupils, relatively older than their classmates, who have been kept back in all their studies by disadvantages, but who, under more favorable circumstances, quickly recover their lost ground, and hence require a change in their classification.

99. The individuality of pupils.—One of the objections most frequently urged against graded-schools is the tendency to crush out all natural individuality—to produce a dead uniformity in tastes, abilities, aspirations, character. If this is the actual result of the graded system of instruction, or even if there is developed a decided tendency to produce such a result, the system is unnatural, and therefore to be condemned. But will some one tell us how the innate individuality of a child can be smothered? If such a result can be accomplished anywhere, it must be in the family, under the persistent influence of parental training. Is it possible to train a family of children, born with different abilities, temperaments, and characters into a sameness of ability, temperament, and character? It is as rational to expect that a family of children, fed with the same food for a succession of years, will adopt an unnatural sameness of physical growth. The fact is, innate differences in character, in ability, in mental habit, will not be ignored, will persist in spite of any training to which they are subjected. The utmost that can be done is to modify individual peculiarities to such a degree as to make human association possible and mutually profitable.

100. Reclassification may be avoided.—Of the reclassifications of pupils which occur in graded-schools, the greater number are downwards, made necessary chiefly by absence or indolence. When a school is in a healthy condition, this redistribution of pupils does not take place spasmodically, at a crisis, but is gradual and unobtrusive, creating no marked impression and leaving no tangible proof of its existence. In other words, that sifting of pupils which is thought so necessary should be done gradually during the year, and not *en masse* at its close. If a graded course of instruction is administered by competent teachers, the pupils who remain in a grade till the close of the year will, as a rule, be competent to enter a higher grade without a formal and formidable examination. The teacher who has heard the daily recitations of a pupil for a year, can pronounce, in advance, a juster opinion of his ability than can be formed by another after an exhaustive examination. I regard the formal examination of pupils at the end of the year, attended with its usual circumstance and ceremony, as a veritable crisis, dangerous to that even tenor which is characteristic of health and normal growth. The process of recitation is in fact an examination in what the pupil has learned for the day from his text-book; and at intervals this examination should be extended to what has been learned for several days, with a view to refresh the pupil's knowledge and to be sure that he is making real progress. By this means, whenever the teacher discovers that a pupil is losing ground and is no longer able to hold his position in the class, he should be reported for a reclassification. Of course, some stimulus is necessary in order to incite the average pupil to improve his opportunities; but it is desirable that this stimulus should be continuous and moderate, not spasmodic and excessive. The normal energies of the pupil should not remain quiescent for the greater part of the year, and then be aroused for a desperate struggle at the end. Some means should be used to convince pupils that the chief end of study is not to be able to "pass;" and I see no surer way than to withdraw the attention somewhat from the impending crisis and fix it more firmly on the fact that each day's work will tell on the final result.

101. Final examinations not a fair test. — It can not have escaped the attention of any who are practically acquainted with school affairs, that in a formal examination, when there is feverish anxiety as to the result, the pupils who are unmistakably the best prepared sometimes acquit themselves with the least credit; while, for a wonder, some whose daily record is an offense, shine with unnatural splendor. Is it just that the promotion of a pupil should be made to depend exclusively, or even very largely, on the chances of an unusual examination? Should his every day work during the year go for nothing? It would be wrong to infer from what has been said that final examinations should be abolished. The thought which is intended to be conveyed is that examinations should not be extraordinary occasions, veritable crises in a pupil's history, obstructing for a time the usual course of school affairs; but rather the last terms of an ordinary series of events, a general summary of the year's results. The fitness of a pupil to enter upon a higher course of study really depends to a considerable extent on his health, industry, punctuality, and general mental habits; and these are concretely represented in the average quality and quantity of work which he has already done.

102. Estimating final standing. — In the case of pupils who are to have a final written examination, a careful record of each recitation and of each monthly examination should be kept, and at the end of the year an average of these results, estimating the average of all the recitations at four-fifths, and the average of all the examinations at one-fifth, should constitute the pupil's standing for the year.

EXAMPLE.

Average of recitations	8.5
Average of monthly examinations	8.

Standing for the year $\frac{4(8.5)+8}{5} = 8.4$

In estimating the final standing, the pupil's standing for the year should be estimated at four-fifths, and the average value of the examination papers at one-fifth.

EXAMPLE.

Standing for the year	8.4
Average value of examination papers	9.

Final standing $\frac{4(8.4)+9}{5} = 8.52$

The relative value which should be assigned to the two items which determine a pupil's final standing is somewhat arbitrary, and each examiner must decide this question for himself.

103. Deciding on fitness for promotion. — With reference to promotion, certain studies may be considered as outranking others. For example, if a pupil is well qualified in arithmetic, grammar, and geography, no teacher would be justifiable in withholding promotion because he is not a fluent reader, or because his penmanship and spelling are defective to a moderate extent. These deficiencies will not bar his progress in the higher grade, but may be repaired there; while an imperfect knowledge of arithmetic and grammar may make further progress impossible. For it should not be forgotten that in deciding on fitness for promotion the real question is, Can this pupil take up the studies of the next grade and pursue them successfully?

Reading, as heretofore defined (§ 49), is a most important acquisition; and a pupil who excels in this art should be very favorably regarded. For, after all, study is but attentive reading; and pupils differ from each other very largely in their respective ability to comprehend the thought of the author as expressed on the printed page. But elocution, or very fine reading, like extraordinary skill in penmanship, sometimes indicates a lack of average mental ability.

A fictitious value is often assigned to excellence in spelling. Poor spelling is not inconsistent with high scholarship. Some learn to spell intuitively and are incapable of misspelling a word; while others, not endowed with great mechanical memory, can never become good spellers. The first are not to be praised nor the last blamed for what they can not prevent. Let it be understood that only the relative values of two different orders of knowledge are in question here. Not the least pretext is given for denying to elocution, penmanship, and spelling a normal amount of attention. The time which, in the writer's opinion, should be given to writing and spelling in a graded course of instruction may be seen by consulting the courses of study as presented on pages 96 and 105.

104. Rigor in examinations. — It should be kept in mind that no unusual rigor in examinations by the superintendent can offset poor instruction by the regular teacher. The true point of departure is the teacher's fitness to instruct. The superintendent is chiefly responsible for the quality of the instruction which pupils receive. His first care should be to secure good teaching ability, and then to direct such methods of instruction as will secure the desired results. Teachers should be held responsible for the fitness of their pupils to leave one point of a graded course and enter on another. The evident fact is that the teacher is in a position to form a more correct judgment on this question than any one else. If the teacher's judgment is not trustworthy; if through favoritism or sympathy, she recommends the promotion of unworthy pupils, she should give place to one who can be trusted. The employment of a teacher is of itself an evidence of confidence in her ability; but a personal inspection of her work in teaching should justify or condemn this confidence. The examination of pupils for promotion, then, should be left almost entirely with teachers who are known to be competent and trustworthy. The superintendent should act in this case, as in all others which relate to the management of pupils, indirectly.

105. Oral and written examinations.—Between the two modes of examination, known as oral and written, there are some differences which are worthy of notice. In general, pupils who recite by "question and answer" should be examined orally, while pupils who recite by "topic" should write out their examination. An oral examination will test the quantity of a pupil's knowledge, a written examination its quality. "Writing maketh an exact man."

Younger pupils are chiefly occupied in receiving knowledge, as distinguished from reproducing the knowledge which has been acquired. It is only by interrogation that the mere child will be able to reveal the extent of his information derived from books, while the older pupil, having learned the art of expression, and having to a greater or less extent made a classification of his knowledge, will be able to give an exact statement of what he knows on an assigned topic.

When pupils have learned to express their thoughts in writing with tolerable grammatical accuracy, a beginning may be made in written examinations, but they should not supersede the usual oral examination. This period is usually the sixth year of the graded course of instruction (§ 53).

During the eighth year, written examinations should occur at intervals, while in the high school they should be employed with considerable frequency.

An incidental advantage of written examinations is the comparison of results which is afforded by them. Take the case of two grammar schools in which pupils are to be examined for promotion to the high school. The same topics being assigned to each school, and the papers being marked in a uniform plan, a very fair estimate can be made of the respective merits of the teachers from a general average of all the results in each case.

Still further, these papers may serve a good purpose as tangible proofs of a pupil's capacity or incapacity, as the case may be. When promotions are withheld the justness of the decision may be called in question, and if so, it will be convenient to produce the records which tell their own story.

106. Conducting a written examination.—In conducting a written examination for promotion from one department to another, the following plan is suggested: Let the teacher assign to each pupil a number by which his papers may be distinguished. Let these numbers be written consecutively on the left margin of the "Examination Roll." Opposite each of these numbers, in the appropriate column, place each pupil's "yearly standing." This list should then be placed in the care of the person who is to decide on the final results. The examination questions should be written on the board, a part at a time, and the pupil should be required to write the answers neatly and legibly. When the papers have been finished they should be folded in a uniform manner, and marked with the name of the topic and the number of the pupil. Let this course be pursued with each topic, and when the examination is finished the papers should be valued with the utmost exactness. For the sake of securing the greatest uniformity in marking, all the papers should be examined by the same person; but where this is impracticable, there should be an agreement on the general plan of marking. Usually, it is not best for a teacher to examine the papers written by her own pupils. The examiner ought not to know the ownership of a single paper.

Each answer should be marked at its estimated value; and the sum of all the marks divided by the number of questions will give the average value of the paper. Mark this value on the paper, and when all the papers on a given topic have been examined, transfer these values to their appropriate place on the "Examination Roll." To find each pupil's standing, proceed as follows: First, find the average value of each pupil's papers by dividing the sum of the several values by the number of papers. Place this average value in its designated place. Then multiply the yearly standing by 4, add to this product the average of the examinations, and divide the sum by 5. The quotient will represent the final standing of the pupil.

Example.

$$\left.\begin{array}{ll}\text{Arithmetic} & 7.5\\ \text{Grammar} & 9.2\\ \text{Geography} & 8.1\\ \text{History} & 7.\end{array}\right\} = 31.8. \quad \text{Average} = \frac{31.8}{4} = 7.95$$

Examination average	7.95
Yearly standing	8.2

$$\text{Final standing} \quad \frac{4(8.2) + 7.95}{5} = \frac{40.75}{5} = 8.15$$

The "Examination Roll," filled out as above directed, will appear as on page 193, supposing that the standard for "passing" is 7.5.

THE PUBLIC SCHOOLS OF ____________

Grammar Grade. *Central School.* *June* 21, 1875.

EXAMINATION ROLL.

No.	Names of Pupils.	Yearly Standing.	Age.	Reading.	Spelling.	Writing.	Arithmetic.	Geography.	Grammar.	U. S. History.		Average of Examination.	Final Standing.	Remarks.
1		8.2	13.				7.1	4.1	10.	7.		7.	8.	Passed.
2		7.5	12.				8.2	7.1	9.	8.		8.1	7.6	Passed.
3		9.1	14.				5.	9.	8.7	7.5		7.6	8.8	Passed.
4		8.7	11.				6.4	4.	7.	6.5		6.	8.2	Passed.
5		7.	15.				9.2	8.	7.7	8.1		8.3	7.4	
6		9.6	14.				10.	9.5	9.7	9.		9.6	9.6	Passed.
7		8.3	13.				8.5	7.6	8.7	7.9		8.2	8.3	Passed.
8		9.	12.				4.	8.	9.1	7.3		7.1	8.6	Passed.
9		7.8	16.				5.6	7.	6.4	5.3		6.1	7.5	Passed.
10		9.7	14.				6.7	8.	9.1	7.8		7.9	9.3	Passed.
	Averages	8.5	13.4				7.	7.2	8.5	7.4		7.6	8.3	

____________ Examiner. ____________ Teacher.

At this stage of proceedings the roll is to be sent back to the teacher, who should write each pupil's name opposite his number. The final results are ready to be declared.

Pupils who have failed in such an examination should be allowed the privilege of another examination at the close of the vacation; but the second examination should be especially searching in those studies where the greatest weakness has been shown. On the one hand, no slavery to mere system should stand in the way of a pupil's efforts to retrieve a failure in the regular examination; and, on the other, there should be no mere trifling in such matters. It must be only in very rare cases that a third examination is allowable.

107. High school examinations.—In the high school, as has already been remarked, greater prominence should be given to written examinations. They should take a wider range, and should be conducted with more system and exactness. A special aim in this department should be to cultivate accurate thinking and the accurate expression of thought. In other words, great prominence should be given to reproducing the knowledge which has been derived from text-book and teacher. Writing necessarily involves a classification of knowledge, each topic being a nucleus about which are grouped facts of a kindred nature. Scholarship consists in having a classified knowledge, such a systematic grouping of facts as will enable their possessor on occasion to produce all the facts which bear on a given subject. This process of classification should at least be begun in the high school; and written examinations should have this for one of their purposes. A very great evil in high school management is the multiplication of studies whereby the whole mental effort of the pupil is expended in memorizing facts which lie in the mind as a *rudis indigestaque moles.*

No degree of true culture can be acquired under such circumstances. The mind must have some leisure to digest the facts which books and teachers supply.

In this grade, then, examinations should promote culture, and they should be so frequent as to divest them of all formality. At the end of each month there should be an examination on all the work done during this period; and at the end of each term, an examination on the term's work; and, finally, at the completion of a study, an examination on the whole subject.

108. Rules for a system of examinations.—To give regularity and efficiency to such a system of examinations, the following plan is suggested:—Faithfully and discretely employed it will be found to produce results which are highly satisfactory.

Rules for a System of Examinations.

Monthly Examinations.

1. The monthly examination shall be estimated as $\frac{1}{4}$, and the average of recitations as $\frac{3}{4}$ in estimating monthly standing.

Example.

Monthly examination, 9.

Average of recitations, 8.5

Monthly standing, $\frac{9 + 3(8.5)}{4} = 8.62$

2. Any pupil falling below the required standing (7.5), for two consecutive months, shall be dismissed from the class.

Term Examinations.

3. The term examination shall be estimated as $\frac{1}{2}$, and the average monthly standing as $\frac{1}{2}$ in calculating a pupil's term standing.

EXAMPLE.

Average monthly standing,	8.2
Term examination,	7.8
Term standing,	$= \frac{8.2 + 7.8}{2} = 8.$

4. When a pupil's term standing falls below 7.5, he shall be dismissed from the class.

Final Examinations.

5. On leaving a text-book, pupils shall be examined on the whole subject; and the average of this examination shall be estimated as ½, and the average term standing as ½ in calculating a pupil's final standing.

EXAMPLE.

Average term standing,	8.6
Average of final examinations,	8.
Final standing,	$= \frac{8.6 + 8}{2} = 8.3$

6. The standard for passing a study shall be 7.5.

7. Pupils shall be granted one reëxamination if application is made within two days from notification of failure.

When pupils fall below the requirements of either of the above rules, and are therefore in danger of falling out of a class, a notice like that on the opposite page should be sent to the parent.

When a study has been completed, it is well to furnish the pupil with some evidence of the fact. It is not only a source of satisfaction to the pupil, but may be needed subsequently to establish the fact of his having passed the study. The form of certificate suggested is on page 198.

______________HIGH SCHOOL.

______________187

*Mr.*______________

*The progress of your*______________

______________ *in* ______________ *for the past month has not been satisfactory, as will be seen from the following record:*

Average of recitations . . . . ______

Monthly examination . . . . . ______

Monthly standing . . . . . . ______

The standard in marking recitations is 10*; and when a pupil's monthly standing in a study falls below* 7.5, *for two consecutive months, he is not allowed to continue such study. The monthly standing is based on the recitations and the examination.*

Very respectfully,

______________ PRINCIPAL.

______HIGH SCHOOL.

THIS CERTIFIES *That* ______ *has completed the study of* ______ *and has passed a satisfactory examination.*

______ 187

______ Teacher.

______ Principal.

Approved by ______ Superintendent.

109. **Deception in examinations.**—Written examinations afford facilities for deception, and the utmost caution should be observed in conducting them. The ways of deception are as various as the inventive power of pupils. A text-book or a leaf smuggled into the class-room, memoranda on bits of paper, on sleeve-cuff, or even on finger nails, memories refreshed by interviews in the halls, these are but specimens of the means which dishonest pupils will take to rob themselves of their rights. It is greatly to be regretted that so loose a code of morals exists in schools; but the evil should be recognized and guarded against by every available resource. To begin at the beginning, an effort should be made to show pupils the inherent immorality of this species of deception; next, the opportunity to deceive should be taken away; and finally, pupils who persist in the practice should be suspended from the privileges of the school.

110. Herbert Spencer on examinations.—The preparation of suitable examination questions is a matter of extreme difficulty as well as of extreme importance. Sometimes a pupil's failure in an examination is due not so much to his own ignorance as to that of his examiners. On this general subject the following extract from Chapter V of Spencer's Study of Sociology is commended to the reader:

"Some months ago, a correspondent of the *Times*, writing from Calcutta, said:

"The Calcutta University examinations of any year would supply curious material for reflection on the value of our educational systems. The prose test in the entrance examination this year includes 'Ivanhoe.' Here are a few of the answers which I have picked up. The spelling is bad, but that I have not cared to give.

"Question: 'Dapper man?' (answer 1) 'Man of superfluous knowledge.' (a. 2) 'Mad.' (q.) 'Democrat?' (a. 1) 'Petticoat government.' (a. 2) 'Witchcraft.' (a. 3) 'Half-turning of the horse.' (q.) 'Babylonish jargon?' (a. 1) 'A vessel made at Babylon.' (a. 2) 'A kind of drink made at Jerusalem.' (a. 3) 'A kind of coat worn by Babylonians.' (q.) 'Lay brother?' (a. 1) 'A bishop.' (a. 2) 'A step-brother.' (a. 3) 'A scholar of the same god-father.' (q.) 'Sumpter mule?' (a.) 'A stubborn Jew.' (q.) 'A bilious-looking fellow?' (a. 1) 'A man of strict character.' (a. 2) 'A person having a nose like the bill of an eagle.' (q.) 'Cloister?' (a.) 'A kind of shell.' (q.) 'Tavern politicians?' (a. 1) 'Politicians in charge of the ale-house.' (a. 2) 'Mere vulgars.' (a. 3) 'Managers of the priestly church.' (q.) 'A pair of cast-off galigaskins?' (a.) 'Two gallons of wine.'

"The fact here drawn attention to as significant is, that these Hindu youths, during their matriculation examination, betrayed so much ignorance of the meanings of words and expressions contained in an English work they had read. And the intended implication appears to be that they were proved to be unfit to begin their college career. If, now, instead of accepting that which is presented to us, we look a little below it, that which may strike us as more noteworthy is the amazing folly of an examiner who proposes to test the fitness of youths for commencing their higher education by seeing how much they knew of the technical terms, cant-phrases, slang, and even extinct slang, talked by the people of another nation. Instead of the unfitness of the boys, which is pointed out to us, we may see rather the unfitness of those concerned in educating them.

"If, again, not dwelling on the particular fact underlying the one offered to our notice, we consider it along with others of the same class, our attention is arrested by the general fact that examiners, and more especially those appointed under our recent systems of administration, habitually put questions a large proportion of which are utterly inappropriate. As I learn from his son, one of our judges not long since found himself unable to answer an examination paper that had been put before law-students. A well-known Greek scholar, editor of a Greek play, who was appointed examiner, found that the examination paper set by his predecessor was too difficult for him. Mr. Froude, in his inaugural address at St. Andrews, describing a paper set by an examiner in English history, said, 'I could myself have answered two questions out of a dozen.' And I learn from Mr. G. H. Lewes that he could not give replies to the questions on English literature which the Civil Service examiners had put to his son. Joining which testimonies, with kindred ones coming from students and professors on all sides, we find the really noteworthy thing to be, that examiners are concerned not so much to set questions fit for students, as to set questions which make manifest their own extensive learning. Especially if they are young, and have reputations to make or to justify, they seize the occasion for displaying their erudition, regardless of the interests of those they examine.

"If we look through this more significant and general fact for the still deeper fact it grows out of, there rises before us the question—Who examines the examiners? How happens it that men, competent in their special knowledge, but so incompetent in their general judgment, should occupy the places they do? This prevailing faultiness of the examiners shows conclusively that the administration is faulty at its center. Somehow or other, the power of ultimate decision is exercised by those who are unfit to exercise it. If the examiners of the examiners were set to fill up an examination paper which had for its subject the right conduct of examinations, and the proper qualifications for examiners, there would come out very unsatisfactory answers.

"Having seen through the small details and the wider facts down to these deeper facts, we may, on contemplating them, perceive that these, too, are not the deepest or most significant. It becomes clear that those having supreme authority suppose, as men in general do, that the sole essential thing for a teacher or examiner is complete knowledge of that which he has to teach, or respecting which he has to examine; whereas a co-essential thing is a knowledge of psychology, and especially of that part of psychology which deals with the evolution of the faculties. Unless, either by special study, or by daily observation and quick insight, he has gained an approximatively true conception of how minds perceive, and reflect, and generalize, and by what processes their ideas grow from concrete to abstract, and from simple to complex, no one is competent to give lessons that will effectually teach, or to ask questions which will effectually measure the efficiency of teaching.

"Further, it becomes manifest that, in common with the public at large, those in authority assume that the goodness of education is to be tested by the quantity of knowledge acquired; whereas it is to be much more truly tested by the capacity for using knowledge — by the extent to which the knowledge gained has been turned into faculty, so as to be available both for the purposes of life and for the purposes of independent investigation."

111. **The preparation of questions.**— In the preparation of examination questions, the following principles should be observed:

1. Their purpose should be to test the accuracy and extent of the pupil's knowledge; and not to display the wisdom, shrewdness, or sagacity of the examiner.

2. They should be pertinent; they should relate to these subjects upon which the pupil has been instructed, and of which his knowledge is to be tested.

3. They should be expressed in terms which the pupil can readily understand.

4. They should be comprehensive in proportion to the degree of mental culture possessed by the pupil.

5. Each question in a series should embrace about the same amount of matter.

The Rhode Island *Schoolmaster* is authority for the statement that the following questions in history were propounded at an examination of teachers:

"1. What is your opinion of the age of the world?

"2. State the reasons for considering the first chapter of Genesis a true history?

"3. How many questions and answers are there in the assembly's shorter catechism?

"Where was Job when God laid the foundation of the earth if the world is round?

"What church do you belong to?"

Questions of this irrelevant nature need only to be stated in order to be shunned; but they are illustrations of a fault which is not peculiar to New England.

"What is the square root of 1225?"

This is a suitable question for pupils who have received their first instruction in higher arithmetic.

"Extract the square root of 1225, and explain the principles involved in the process."

This is adapted to the capacities of pupils more advanced, who have been taught the science of arithmetic.

"Demonstrate the general theorem of roots."

This implies a still higher knowledge of mathematics, and is suitable for advanced pupils in algebra.

(1) "Through what waters must one pass in sailing from Chicago to London?

(2) "Name the large rivers in South America.

(3) "What is the capital of France?"

Such a series of questions, involving such unequal amounts of information, does not afford a fair test of the relative abilities of pupils. Three pupils answering only the first, second, and third, respectively, would receive the same credit; when it is evident that these credits should be at least as five, two, and one.

On the same principle, three series of questions, each having reference to a different topic, as arithmetic, grammar, and history, should each embrace about an equal amount of matter; otherwise, a general average of the three sets of papers might not represent the relative merits of different pupils.

The answers given to examination questions may be complete or incomplete; correct, partially correct, or incorrect. An answer may be incomplete, though correct as far as it goes; or it may be partly correct and partly incorrect. In marking papers these facts should be taken into account. A pupil should be credited with whatever knowledge of the subject he embodies in his examination papers.

"For twelve dollars, how many books can be bought at two-thirds of a dollar each?" Answer 1. "You can buy as many books as two-thirds of twelve, which is eight." Answer 2. "You can buy as many books as two-thirds is contained in twelve. To divide a whole number by a fraction, multiply by the denominator and divide by the numerator. $3 \times 12 = 36$; $36 \div 2 = 18$. Hence you can buy 18 books." Answer 3. "For $12 there can be bought as many books as ⅔, the price of one book, is contained in 12. 1 is contained in 12, twelve times; ⅓ is contained in 12 thirty-six times; ⅔ is contained in 12 eighteen times. Hence eighteen books can be bought for $12 at ⅔ of a dollar each."

The first answer indicates complete ignorance of the subject, and should be marked 0.

The second answer is correct, but it indicates a mere knowledge of the rule for the division of an integer by a fraction. It may be marked 7.5.

The third answer shows that the pupil knows what to do, how to do it, and why he does it. It indicates a complete knowledge of the subject in hand, and should be marked 10.

"How does respiration purify the blood?" Answer 1. "The oxygen of the air deprives the blood of its impurities."

This answer is correct, though incomplete. It gives evidence of a knowledge of the fact in the case, but does not exhibit any understanding of the process which really takes place. If this reply were to be given in an examination in physiology or chemistry, it should not be marked above 5.

Answer 2. "The oxygen of the air combines with the carbon of the blood, which is one of its impurities, and expels the poisonous hydrogen."

Here the general fact expressed in the first answer seems to be known; but the account of the process is both incomplete and partially incorrect. This answer should not be marked above 6.

Answer 3. "The chief impurities in the blood are compounds of carbon and hydrogen. The oxygen of the air combines with the first, forming carbonic acid, and with the second, producing watery vapor. These gases, along with the nitrogen contained in the inspired air, are expelled from the lungs in the process of breathing."

This reply may be marked 9 or 10, depending on whether the examination is in chemistry or physiology.

In a mathematical examination, where the purpose is to test a pupil's knowledge of processes or of principles, mere errors in calculation, arising through inadvertance, should not be taken into account.

These illustrations sufficiently indicate the principles which should be observed in the preparation and marking of examination papers designed to test a pupil's fitness for promotion.

112. Examinations to develop general principles.—Written examinations serve a secondary purpose of great importance. They assist pupils in understanding isolated facts—in introducing order into their mental acquisitions—in classifying their knowledge. A pupil may know the several facts which underlie a general principle; he may repeat the abstract formula which really includes these very facts, and yet he may be wholly unable to detect the individual cases which fall under the general law. To understand a fact, is to see it in its relations to other facts and to the whole of which they are the several parts. Pupils should be assisted in discovering these relations; and judicious questions are often the only aid which it is possible to render.

In the illustration of these remarks, let us take the case of pupils who do not understand the atomic theory, that is, do not see in this theory the ascertained facts of chemical combination in their relation to one another. What is needed is to bring these facts into sharp outline, and, at the same time, into suggestive relations, so that the mind may discover a unity in phenomena which before seemed isolated facts. An examination paper, set in the following form, will often lead to a better understanding of a somewhat difficult subject:

1. Of what *elements* is HCl composed?

2. If we were to decompose *two quarts* of HCl, what volume of H would result; what volume of Cl?

3. If we were to form 1,000 cubic inches of HCl by a synthesis of its elements, what volume of each *must* we take?

4. In making this combination, if we were to take less than the required volume of H by *one cubic inch*, what amount of Cl would remain free? How many cubic inches of HCl would be formed?

5. If we were to decompose a given *weight* of HCl, what relative *weights* of the elementary gases would result? What relative *volumes* of H and Cl would result?

6. What, then, are the *specific weights* of H and Cl, respectively; what are their *atomic weights?*

7. If we were to form a given *weight* of HCl by a syn-

thesis of its elements, what *relative* weights of H and Cl *must* we take?

8. In making this combination, if we were to take less than the required weight of H by *one grain*, what *weight* of Cl would remain free?

9. What, then, are the *combining weights* of H and Cl, respectively?

This process is not prescribed as a panacea for all ills of this class; but, like all good remedies, discreetly employed, it will be found in many cases to answer a valuable purpose.

113. **Public examinations.**—Besides the examinations for the purpose of reclassifying pupils, there is another purpose for which a different manner of examining is necessary. At least once in each year, the schools should be thrown open to the general public, to the end that the actual condition of the schools may be observed. It is right in itself that the people should know with what success the system is administered; and it is often of the greatest advantage to a school to receive the candid criticisms which intelligent citizens may see occasion to make. It is to be recollected that faults which may escape a teacher's notice may be detected at a glance by others who occupy a different point of view.

To make such examinations effective, committees should be appointed by the Board of Education, composed of intelligent citizens who feel an active interest in the schools and will be likely to form a dispassionate judgment of them. These committees should be requested to furnish the Board with frank statements of opinion respecting points on which improvements can be made. Such criticisms may be anonymous, so far as the individual members of the committees are concerned. There might be a hesitation in making a frank expression of opinion, if it were necessary to appear by name in connection with an adverse criticism.

On the occasion of such examinations, the schools should appear in their every-day dress. What the public wish to observe is the ordinary work which is done in the schools. Every necessary precaution should therefore be used to prevent any display prepared for the occasion. The usual programme should be followed with no variations save such as the committees may desire to make. Teachers should be enjoined to present only fair specimens of their work; and any attempt to create a display for the occasion should be sufficient cause to forfeit one's position.

Preparatory to this examination, programmes should be prepared indicating the time and place of each examination. If different committees are appointed for each grade and building, these public examinations may be held simultane-

No. XXVI.

The Public Schools of ______________________

Superintendent's Office, ______________________ 187

M. ______________________

You have been appointed by the Board of Education a member of a Committee for examining Schools; and you will confer a favor by acting in this capacity. Information as to time and place will be found in the inclosed schedule.

Respectfully,

______________________ SUPT.

ously; for example, on Tuesday, Wednesday, and Thursday of the last week in the second term of the year. A copy of the programme, with a notice similar to the preceding, should be sent to each member of the committees.

Some plan like the foregoing is one of the surest means to create and sustain a public opinion favorable to our public school system. The schools belong to the people, and they will prosper just in proportion as the people feel a confidence in their utility and in the honesty of purpose and general success with which they are conducted.

INDEX.

(*The numbers refer to pages.*)

www.ingramcontent.com/pod-product-compliance
Lightning Source LLC
LaVergne TN
LVHW011203110826
845150LV00006B/1308
* 9 7 8 1 4 2 5 5 1 8 5 9 2 *